EVER SINCE PARADISE

*An Entertainment chiefly referring
to Love and Marriage*

In Three Acts
by
J. B. PRIESTLEY

With Music
by
DENNIS ARUNDELL

SAMUEL FRENCH LIMITED
LONDON

Copyright © 1946 by J.B. Priestley
All Rights Reserved

EVER SINCE PARADISE is fully protected under the copyright laws of the British Commonwealth, including Canada, the United States of America, and all other countries of the Copyright Union. All rights, including professional and amateur stage productions, recitation, lecturing, public reading, motion picture, radio broadcasting, television and the rights of translation into foreign languages are strictly reserved.

ISBN 978-0-573-11651-3
www.samuelfrench.co.uk
www.samuelfrench.com

For Amateur Production Enquiries

United Kingdom and World
excluding north america
plays@samuelfrench.co.uk
020 7255 4302/01

Each title is subject to availability from Samuel French, depending upon country of performance.

CAUTION: Professional and amateur producers are hereby warned that *EVER SINCE PARADISE* is subject to a licensing fee. Publication of this play does not imply availability for performance. Both amateurs and professionals considering a production are strongly advised to apply to the appropriate agent before starting rehearsals, advertising, or booking a theatre. A licensing fee must be paid whether the title is presented for charity or gain and whether or not admission is charged.

The Professional Rights in this play are controlled by United Agents LLP, 12-26 Lexington St, Soho, London W1F 0LE.

No one shall make any changes in this title for the purpose of production. No part of this book may be reproduced, stored in a retrieval system, or transmitted in any form, by any means, now known or yet to be invented, including mechanical, electronic, photocopying, recording, videotaping, or otherwise, without the prior written permission of the publisher. No one shall upload this title, or part of this title, to any social media websites.

The right of J.B. Priestley to be identified as author of this work has been asserted in accordance with Section 77 of the Copyright, Designs and Patents Act 1988.

EVER SINCE PARADISE

Produced at the New Theatre, London, W.C.2, on June 4th, 1947, with the following cast of characters—

(in the order of their appearance)

PHILIP	*Dennis Arundell.*
JOYCE	*Jane Carr.*
WILLIAM	*Roger Livesey.*
HELEN .	*Ursula Jeans.*
ROSEMARY	*Joy Shelton.*
PAUL	*Hugh Kelly.*

The Play produced by the Author.

The action is in many different places, and the time is the present.

EVER SINCE PARADISE

ACT I

The main curtain may or may not be used, according to the size of the stage. On each side of the stage, as far apart as possible, is a grand piano, each exactly alike. A little on stage from each piano are two stools, one each for use of the commentators. This setting is backed by a further curtained proscenium front, concealing an inner stage, which extends in the form of an apron or rostrum a few feet below the second curtain line. R. *and* L. *of the second proscenium are curtained arches.*

(See the Ground Plan at the end of the play.)

When the CURTAIN *rises, the inner Curtains and Arch-curtains are closed. Lights Cue* I. PHILIP *in dinner jacket is seated playing the piano* R. *and* JOYCE, *also in evening dress, is seated playing the piano* L. *They are two youngish people, and commence playing the overture—Music Cue* I, *shortly before the* CURTAIN *rises. The overture continues for about two or three minutes after the rise of the* CURTAIN, *both keeping perfect time. Then they begin to sound ragged and to look worried.* PHILIP *wants to increase the tempo and* JOYCE *is lagging behind. Finally, with a discordant crash, they stop playing, and glare across at each other.*

PHILIP (*rising angrily*). There 'you are, you see!
JOYCE (*rising angrily and moving* L.C.). It's not my fault.
PHILIP (*moving* R.C.). Of course it is.
JOYCE. No, it isn't, it's your fault.
PHILIP. No, it isn't, you were dragging it again.
JOYCE. I wasn't. You were racing away at a ridiculous pace.
PHILIP. I wasn't.
JOYCE. You were. Always the same! Want to rush everything.
PHILIP. I don't want to rush everything.
JOYCE. Yes, you do. Going and taking that cottage!
PHILIP (*very angrily*). What's my taking that cottage got to do with your dragging the time again——?

(WILLIAM, *in dinner jacket, enters* L. *and moves down* C.)

WILLIAM (*reproachfully*). I say, I say, this won't do, you know. You two ought to be playing, not shouting at each other. (*To the audience.*) I'm so sorry about this. Do excuse us,

please! (*To* PHILIP *and* JOYCE.) You were playing so well, too. I was just remarking to Helen how well you were playing—and then—no more music but another quarrel.
JOYCE. It's his fault. He began to rush it again.
WILLIAM. Now, Philip, you mustn't rush it——
PHILIP. I wasn't. She *will* drag it. (*He breaks to the piano* R. *and sits at it.*)
WILLIAM (*turning to* JOYCE). Now, Joyce, you really mustn't drag it——
JOYCE. I never do. That's just his stupidity.
PHILIP (*rising angrily*). It isn't. It's your——
WILLIAM (*very forcefully*). Stop it, stop it, stop it!

(JOYCE *breaks to the piano* L.)

Now if one of you would condescend to rush a little less——

(PHILIP *and* JOYCE *sit at their pianos.*)

—then no doubt you'd keep together, be in time—— (*He breaks to* L.C.)

(HELEN, *in a simple but striking evening dress, enters* R., *moves to the piano* R. *and leans on the upstage end of it.*)

—in exquisite unison, in beautiful harmony, and you'd both be happy and we'd be happy. Whereas . . .
HELEN. William, you always go on too long.
WILLIAM (*rather annoyed*). How do you mean—I always go on too long?
HELEN. You shouldn't go on with that "whereas". Nobody wants your *whereas*. And it's pompous. You're rather inclined to be pompous, you know.
WILLIAM (*horrified*). Pompous! My dear Helen, I'm the least pompous man who ever lived.
JOYCE. You're *all* pompous.
HELEN. Perfectly true (*she moves* C.), Joyce, dear. They *are* all pompous. But when William has a grievance, I think he's really above the average in pompousness.

(PHILIP *guffaws audibly.*)

WILLIAM (*glaring across at* PHILIP). If you're going to snigger and provide her with an appreciative audience, she'll go on for hours.
HELEN. Audience! (*She breaks to down* R.C.) That reminds me. (*To the audience, with tremendous charm.*) I'm so sorry about all this. Do excuse us, please.
WILLIAM (*moving to* HELEN *and patting her on the shoulder*). I've said that already.
HELEN (*sweetly*). Possibly, but perhaps when a little charm is added to the apology——

WILLIAM (*interrupting her*). Charm! If there's one quality more contemptible than another in our contemptible bag of tricks, it's this famous feminine charm. As soon as I see that rotten little piece of scented silk run up as a flag, I know that honesty and decency are about to be scuttled. (*He breaks* L.)

PHILIP. And I agree.

HELEN (*turning to* PHILIP). Only because you haven't any, Philip dear.

PHILIP. Oh—I don't know about that.

HELEN (*smiling sweetly at* PHILIP). No, Philip, you don't know about it. (*She moves to* R.C.)

WILLIAM (*breaking to* HELEN *and turning her round to face him*). Now what's the matter with you?

HELEN (*with wide-eyed innocence*). Nothing that I know of, William. Why?

WILLIAM. Because you're behaving very badly, that's why. You come on here, looking—I must admit—very delightful, shining and smiling upon us like a May moon——

HELEN. Thank you, my pet.

WILLIAM. I'm not your pet. (*He breaks a little to* C.) And keep away, keep away.

HELEN. Oh—why?

WILLIAM. Because—well it's less confusing and easier for me to say what I have to say——

HELEN (*moving to the stool* R.). Then don't say it. (*She sits.*) Nobody cares.

WILLIAM (*breaking to* L. *of* HELEN). And what I say is that you come on here and instead of trying to help us out of our little difficulty, you at once make everything worse. Now why—why—do you go and make everything worse?

HELEN. Shall I tell you?

WILLIAM (*exasperated*). I'm asking you to tell me. (*He leans over* HELEN.) Though I doubt if you know.

HELEN. Oh, yes, I do. It's perfectly simple. You see, being a woman I must be noticed and appreciated. We take a great deal of trouble over our appearance—(*she adjusts* WILLIAM'S *bow*) about twenty times as much trouble as you do, for instance.

(WILLIAM *breaks to* C.)

And we insist upon first being noticed and appreciated. Now if you'd said, at once, that I was looking very nice, or if you'd only smiled at me, that would have been quite enough. Immediately I'd have felt full of goodwill and kindness and helpfulness, and I'd have tried to do my best for everybody. But first of all I must be noticed and appreciated.

WILLIAM. That seems to me all wrong.

HELEN. Yes, but then you happen to be a man and I happen to be a woman.

WILLIAM. It shouldn't make so much difference.
HELEN. But it does.
WILLIAM. Well, does it? I know women who aren't like that.
HELEN. Yes, and how much time do you spend with them?

(JOYCE *bursts out laughing.*)

WILLIAM (*breaking to the piano* L. *and speaking to* JOYCE). I think you'd better start playing again.

(JOYCE *commences playing—Music Cue 2.*)

HELEN (*rising*). No, not yet. (*She breaks to* R. *of* WILLIAM *at* L.C.)
WILLIAM. Why not?

(JOYCE *ceases playing.*)

HELEN. I think—we ought to look into this a little more. This man-and-woman business.
WILLIAM (*with gloomy approval*). Yes, it needs looking into.
HELEN. Of course it does. (*She moves to* C.) Now it's no use taking ourselves, is it?
WILLIAM (*brightening at this*) Not a bit. (*He turns and moves to the stool* L.) Lot of talk about ourselves—only leads to trouble —scenes, temper and tears—terrible! (*He sits.*) No use, you see, unless you can be detached.
HELEN. You love being detached, don't you?
WILLIAM. Can't observe properly unless you're detached. That's obvious. (*He makes a double take to* JOYCE.)
HELEN. All right, then, we'll take some other pair.
PHILIP. What about Henry and Muriel?
JOYCE. Dull.
WILLIAM (*to* JOYCE). Very dull.
HELEN. I'm afraid you're right. Well, you suggest somebody.
WILLIAM. Boris and Nina.
HELEN. Oh—no, just a long cat-and-dog fight broken by an occasional orgy.
WILLIAM (*thoughtfully*). True. (*He rises and breaks down* C.) Though I've always wanted to be in at an orgy. All this writing and talk about orgies, and yet you never seem to catch up with one. Every place I've ever been to, they've always just stopped having them. " You ought to have been here last year," they say. " It was terrible."
PHILIP. I know.
JOYCE. How do you mean, you know?
WILLIAM (*breaking to the piano* L.). Now, Joyce, don't you two start all over again. Look at your music or something.
HELEN (*triumphantly*). I know the very pair. Not too dull, not too wild. Very nice and rather typical. Paul and Rosemary.

ACT I] EVER SINCE PARADISE 5

WILLIAM (*breaking to* HELEN). Rosemary and Paul. Yes, they might do. Pleasant pair. As you say, nice people. Not very intelligent perhaps, but I can supply the intelligence.

HELEN (*closing to* R. *of* WILLIAM). And you've heard what's happening to them?

WILLIAM. No. Not busting up, are they?

HELEN (*leading* WILLIAM *to the stool* L.). Sit down and pay attention.

(WILLIAM *sits and turns towards the inner stage.*)

You'll see. Joyce, Philip! (*She crosses to the stool* R. *and sits.*)

(JOYCE *and* PHILIP *commence playing some broken, discordant music—Music Cue 3. Lights Cue 2.*)

EPISODE I

The Curtains open to reveal a room whose few props suggest a waiting-room in a solicitor's office.
There is a window R., *a bookcase back* C., *with some deed-boxes* R. *of it. The door is* L. *A chair stands* L.C.
(*See the Ground Plan at the end of the play.*)

PAUL, *in the middle thirties, with horn-rimmed spectacles and wearing a check overcoat and muffler (to facilitate quick change), is moving about, crossing to* L. *and* R., *like a man kept waiting for an unpleasant appointment. After a moment,* ROSEMARY *is heard speaking off* L.

ROSEMARY (*off*). Oh, in here. Thank you!

(ROSEMARY, *also wearing a heavy coat, and looking pale and miserable, enters* L. *She stops and stares at* PAUL *who looks very embarrassed.*)

PAUL (*with an effort, now standing* R.C.). I'm afraid this is—er rather embarrassing—Rosemary.

ROSEMARY (*with a similar effort*). Yes—Paul—I'm afraid it is. (*She moves to the chair, sits and looks away from* PAUL.)

PAUL. Well, it's not my fault . . . I had a note from Coulson asking me to be here at half-past three—to answer some questions about the—the divorce.

ROSEMARY (*with a tiny voice*). Yes, so had I.

PAUL (*restlessly, moving to up* C.). Oh, I say—monstrous thing for Coulson to do—(*he turns*) asking us both here at the same time. Shows you how blankly insensitive these lawyers are. (*He crosses* R. *and turns.*) Typical lawyer's trick, this. Damn Coulson!

ROSEMARY (*faintly*). Oh—I don't think—it's—perhaps . . . (*Her voice dies away.*)

PAUL. What?

ROSEMARY. No—nothing.
PAUL (*closing to* R. *of the chair*). Look here, I'll go and wait out there. (*He indicates the door* L.)
ROSEMARY. No—it . . . (*She makes a movement as if to halt him.*)
PAUL (*moving to the door* L.). Don't mind a bit.

(PAUL *exits* L. ROSEMARY *stares after him a moment, then sinks back in the chair. Her face begins working, and she starts sobbing.*)

WILLIAM (*rising and mounting the rostrum at* L.C.). I say, this is too bad.

(*The Curtains close.* JOYCE *and* PHILIP *play some broken discordant music—Music Cue 3a. Lights Cue 3.* HELEN *rises and mounts the rostrum* R.C.)

Now, Helen.

(WILLIAM *and* HELEN *meet* C. *on the rostrum. She takes his* R. *arm. They break together off the rostrum to down* C. *The Pianists cease playing.*)

HELEN (*sympathetically not satirically*). What made it all the worse, of course, is that obviously it was she who had asked their solicitor to send for them both at the same time.
WILLIAM. Yes, but I—can't see why she should do that if they were arranging a divorce.
HELEN. Because she was hoping that a miracle might have happened, that, seeing her again, he might have discovered he was still in love with her. (*She looks away to* R.) We're always hoping for miracles like that. And then—well, you saw.
WILLIAM. Yes, but, mind you, if he'd been completely indifferent he'd have stayed in there. He went out chiefly for her sake.
HELEN. She thought he went out because he couldn't even stand the sight of her.
WILLIAM (*moving a little down* L.). Quite wrong. (*He turns.*) What a lot of muddlers we are, aren't we ? She ought to be crying over the human race. There *is* something to cry about. (*He eases* L.C.)
HELEN (*very gravely*). She was crying because once there was love and now there is no love. (*She turns while speaking, moves to the stool* R. *and sits.*) If we can't cry over the grave of love, what are our tears for ? I could cry a little myself.
WILLIAM (*crossing to* HELEN ; *anxiously*). Now, now ! Now, now ? Don't you start, my dear. Besides, we must keep our detachment, or we'll never learn anything. (*He addresses the Pianists.*) Play something quiet, but cheerful.

(JOYCE *and* PHILIP *commence to play—Music Cue 4.* HELEN *turns her face to* WILLIAM *and smiles.*)

(*He takes* HELEN'S *hand.*) That's better. (*He pats her hand, releases it, crosses to* R. *of the piano* L. *and turns.*) Let me see now, how did this begin? Where, when and how did Paul and Rosemary first meet?
HELEN (*slowly and reflectively*). She told me once. Her father gave Paul some architectural job and asked him to come and dine.
(*The Pianists cease playing for a few moments.*)
(*She rises and moves* C.) You'll have to be Rosemary's father. Go on!
WILLIAM. I thought for a moment you said I'd have to be Rosemary's father?
HELEN. That's what I did say. Go on.
WILLIAM. Certainly. Great pleasure. (*He moves to the arch* L.) Only not for long, y'know.
(*The Pianists resume playing softly.* WILLIAM *exits* L.)

HELEN (*moving to above the piano* R.). It takes some girls months, some years, before they know, but she seemed to know at once. (*She leans on the piano* R.)

(*The music swells up. Lights Cue 4.*)

EPISODE 2

The Curtains open to reveal a corner of the drawing-room in ROSEMARY'S *home.*
There is a small table C. *On it are a tray with a decanter of sherry and three glasses, an ashtray and a box of cigarettes. There is no other furniture.*
(*See the Ground Plan at the end of the play.*)

ROSEMARY, *looking younger and prettier, is* R. *of the table. She pours out three glasses of sherry.* PAUL, *who looks younger without the spectacles, enters* L., *and moves to* L. *of the table. The Pianists cease playing.* WILLIAM, *wearing a grey wig and moustache as* ROSEMARY'S *father, enters* L. *immediately following* PAUL. WILLIAM *moves to above the table.*

WILLIAM (*speaking in an older man's voice*). Ah—you haven't met my daughter Rosemary, I think. My dear—Mr Paul Weybridge.

(ROSEMARY *and* PAUL *smile and shake hands.*)

Glass of sherry, eh?

(ROSEMARY *hands* PAUL *and* WILLIAM *a glass of sherry each.*)

Thank you, my dear. (*He drinks.*)
ROSEMARY (*smiling at* PAUL). And how's the bungalow?
PAUL (*smiling back at* ROSEMARY). I think it's going to be grand.
ROSEMARY. I thought your idea for it awfully clever.
PAUL. Thank you.

(PAUL *and* ROSEMARY *raise their glasses and drink, at the same time smiling at each other significantly over the top of them.*)

WILLIAM (*rambling on without noticing them*). Yes, yes—I think Weybridge realizes now exactly what I've always had in mind. Convenient and cosy are my two watchwords. Easy and cheap to run, but snug. Plenty of weather outside, on the top of that cliff (*he pours another glass of sherry for himself*), but none inside, eh, Weybridge. (*He drinks.*)
PAUL (*who is lost*). What? Oh—yes, rather—that's the idea.
WILLIAM. Made a little sketch or two I wanted to show you. Have 'em in my den. (*He moves* L., *taking his glass with him.*) This way, my boy.

(WILLIAM *exits* L. JOYCE *and* PHILIP *commence to play softly for a moment or two—Music Cue 4a.* PAUL *hands his glass to* ROSEMARY, *there is a pause between them, then he, obviously reluctant, turns and exits* L. ROSEMARY *stands in a daydream. The Pianists cease playing.* ROSEMARY *places the glasses on the table, then moves forward a pace or two and speaks to* HELEN.)

ROSEMARY. Really I knew then. Or one part of me did.
HELEN (*with sympathy*). I know.
ROSEMARY. That part of me which seems to stand back always and isn't caught up with every moment.
HELEN. Yes, the part that can see far ahead, in a dim sort of way, and seems to know what's coming.
ROSEMARY. That's exactly it, Helen. But how does it work? I mean, it's just as if behind the little *now* there's this big *Now*, in which all at once you've met a man and loved him for years and lost him. And how can that be? (*She turns and moves up stage.*)
HELEN. I don't know, darling. I don't believe anybody knows.

(*The Curtains close. Lights Cue 5.* WILLIAM, *without the wig and moustache, enters briskly through the centre of the curtains on to the rostrum.*)

WILLIAM. I know. It's a question of movement along the fourth dimension—— (*He moves to* R.C. *on the rostrum.*)
HELEN (*breaking to* R. *of* WILLIAM). What is?

Act I] EVER SINCE PARADISE 9

WILLIAM. These two Nows—two different kinds of time. Now imagine yourself travelling with the speed of light—a hundred and eighty-six thousand miles a second—along the fourth dimension——
JOYCE (*rising*). No.
PHILIP (*rising*). No.
HELEN. No, thank you, William.
WILLIAM. I thought you wanted to know.

(JOYCE *and* PHILIP *both sit.*)

HELEN. Not just now, thank you. Some other time. (*She moves to the stool* R. *and sits.*) Now I wonder when Paul realized he was falling in love with Rosemary?
WILLIAM. Does it matter?
HELEN. Of course it matters.
WILLIAM. Well, he told me it was about the third or fourth time he went there. They were just saying good-bye in the hall.

(PHILIP *plays a few notes—Music Cue 4b. Lights Cue 6.* HELEN *waves* WILLIAM *off the rostrum. He breaks to the stool* L. *and sits.*)

EPISODE 3

The Curtains open to reveal the entrance-hall of ROSEMARY'S *home. There is a hall table* C., *with a silver card-tray and a newspaper on it.*
(*See the Ground Plan at the end of the play.*)

PAUL, *dressed in a light overcoat and carrying his hat, is standing* L. *of* ROSEMARY, *about to say good night.* PHILIP *ceases playing.*

ROSEMARY (*lightly*). You know, if your taxi *is* ticking its life away outside, you needn't wait for father. He may be ages digging out that old photograph, but he can easily post it to you. (*She offers her hand shyly.*)

(PAUL *looks nervously off* L. *He turns and offers his hand.* ROSEMARY *withdraws hers.*)

PAUL. Well, the taxi *is* there, so I suppose I'd better go. (*He hesitates, then speaks with a rush.*) I wondered—well, the fact is, I've been working too hard lately to go out much, but a —er—client gave me two seats for the Haymarket for next Thursday, and—er—I wondered—whether you'd like to come along with me. We might have some supper afterwards if you like—and—er—dance.
ROSEMARY (*slowly*). Thursday? Yes, I'd love to.
PAUL. We'll have to meet at the theatre, if you don't mind, as I'm afraid I shan't have time to dine.

ROSEMARY. No, of course not. We can find out what time it begins, can't we?
PAUL. Yes, I don't think they make any secret of that. Well—Thursday then.

(*They shake hands.*)

(*He hesitates.*) I suppose you probably go out nearly every night—with fellows who are rolling in money—but to me Thursday will be quite an occasion.
ROSEMARY (*with apparent calm*). Oh—I'm looking forward to it too.
PAUL. I . . . (*He breaks* L., *then checks himself.*) Good night.

(*He turns and exits* L.)

ROSEMARY (*as he goes*). Good night.

(*There is a short pause. Lights Cue 7.*)

(*She talks with great urgency to herself.*) Thursday, Thursday, Thursday. I'll have to put Alice off, of course, but she won't mind. Also the Kershaws can't come to tea because I may not get back from the hairdresser's in time, but I can easily put them off. Now if I wear my blue I've time to get another belt—and—oh!—some shoes—I'll go down on Wednesday with Alice and buy the shoes. That black bag's filthy but it'll have to do. Unless I can get a blue one—like Alice's—she said it was quite cheap—where was it? Somewhere in Regent Street . . .

(WILLIAM *rises and tries to attract* HELEN'S *attention.*)

I might look at them while I'm getting the shoes. But perhaps after all it might be better to wear the white, though it'll be creased in the theatre and might look terrible afterwards.

(WILLIAM *is still trying to attract* HELEN'S *attention.*)

And that means wearing my rotten old red velvet coat—I might have it cleaned, but they're horribly slow at that place.
WILLIAM. No, no, no.

(*The Curtains close. Lights Cue 8.*)

Can't have any more of that. (*He crosses to* R.C.) Drive a man barmy!

(*He looks at* HELEN, *who is calm and smiling.*)

How long would she go on like that?
HELEN. Hours and hours probably.
WILLIAM. Good God! But the evening she's going to have simply won't be worth all that agonizing. Better to stop at home. (*He closes with* HELEN.)
HELEN. Nonsense!

WILLIAM. Did you go through all that?
HELEN. Certainly—still do, sometimes.
PHILIP (*shaking his head*). Simply isn't worth it.
HELEN. We think it is.
JOYCE. And so—really—do you.
WILLIAM. You know—I believe the secret of you women is—you've got far less individual conceit than we have.
JOYCE }
HELEN } (*together*). But—of course.
JOYCE. That's why we take so much more trouble with ourselves.
WILLIAM (*turning and moving up on to* C. *of the rostrum*). On the other hand, as a sex, you seem to have an enormous collective conceit.
HELEN. How do you mean?
WILLIAM. Well, you're all convinced that though individually you may not be up to much, Woman herself is a tremendous treat. That's why if a man starts falling out of love with one of you, you always believe it's because he's falling *in* love with another one.
JOYCE. And nine times out of ten, at least, we're right!
WILLIAM (*descending from the rostrum, and moving down* C.). It's a sort of trades union conceit. We can't do without a member of the union. And very annoyed you are too when we prove we can.
HELEN (*rising and closing to* R. *of* WILLIAM). When you can ignore us, you've said good-bye to all hope of magic.
WILLIAM. Magic of a kind. Often a witch's brew. But we can do without your magic, because we're all sons of Adam, who did without it once. But you're all the daughters of poor Eve, who was never by herself, but found Adam already there.
HELEN. And ever since Eve we've felt socially responsible, and even as guests we're still anxious hostesses.
PHILIP (*calling out*). Too much talk!

(PHILIP *nods to* JOYCE *and they burst into loud dance music—Music Cue 5.* WILLIAM *turns, moves up stage and with his back to the audience, takes a pair of spectacles from his pocket and puts them on. Then he turns and moves down* C. *The music softens.*)

WILLIAM. Now this is where I might indulge in one of those philosophical disquisitions on Jazz and the Spirit of the Age, which were so popular a few years ago.

(HELEN *breaks to* WILLIAM, *takes off his spectacles and puts them in his breast pocket.*)

HELEN. This *is* a few years ago, but you're not here to philosophize, but to dance.

(*The music swells up. Lights Cue 9.* HELEN *takes* WILLIAM'S
hand and leads him up on to R.C. *of the rostrum.* PAUL, *in dinner
jacket, and* ROSEMARY *in evening dress, enter by the arch* L., *move
up on to* L.C. *of the rostrum. Both couples commence to dance.*)

WILLIAM (*as they dance*). Having a grand time, isn't she?
HELEN. Yes. So is he. Both of 'em just working up to
something drastic. Lovely!
WILLIAM. Might be lovely. (*He pauses.*) Might not. Can't
tell. (*He pauses again.*) Never understand why you women
always want to help on the biological process. Pairing everybody
off as if you were all Mrs Noah and it had started to rain.
HELEN. We know what life's about.
WILLIAM. My pet, you haven't the foggiest idea.

(*The music ceases.* WILLIAM *bumps into* PAUL *at the finish of the
dance.*)

Sorry.

(*They all stop dancing and clap.* PAUL, HELEN *and* ROSEMARY
enthusiastically, WILLIAM *perfunctorily.* HELEN, PAUL *and*
WILLIAM *step down from the rostrum.*)

HELEN. You know William, of course, don't you? Paul,
Rosemary.

(HELEN *and* PAUL *ease* R. *and stand conversing softly.*)

WILLIAM (*standing* C. *and addressing* ROSEMARY). Enjoying
yourself, I can see that.
ROSEMARY (*still on the rostrum at* L.C.). Yes, I am, aren't
you?
WILLIAM. Not much.
ROSEMARY. Oh, what a shame! I like this place. (*She looks
about her happily.*)
WILLIAM (*looking about unhappily*). I don't. It frightens me.
ROSEMARY. Some of the people do look pretty awful.
WILLIAM. And some look awfully pretty. But that's not it.
Consider the social and philosophical background.
ROSEMARY. I don't think I want to very much, tonight.
WILLIAM (*almost as if announcing a lecture*). Jazz, Swing and
the Spirit of the Age.
HELEN (*breaking off her talk with* PAUL). No, William, not
tonight. And the cabaret will be starting soon. Naked young
women.
WILLIAM (*gloomily*). And dirty songs at the piano.

(JOYCE *and* PHILIP *commence to play dance music again softly—
Music Cue 6.* PAUL *breaks to* C. *below the rostrum. He pauses
a moment, looking at* ROSEMARY.)

PAUL (*happily*). Rosemary! (*He holds out his hand.*)

Act I]   EVER SINCE PARADISE

Rosemary (*moving happily to* c. *of the rostrum*).   Yes, Paul.
(*She takes his hand and steps off the rostrum.*)
   Paul. Let's dance.

(Paul *and* Rosemary *commence to dance round about* c. *stage.*
   William *eases up* r., *closing to* Helen.)

   William. What's the matter with 'em now?
   Helen. It's the first time he's ever called her Rosemary, and the first time she's ever called him Paul.

(*The curtains of the arch* l. *open.* Paul *and* Rosemary *smile and wave as they dance off through the arch. The arch curtains close. The Pianists cease playing. Lights Cue 10.*)

And you needn't look so glum about it. That's a very important moment. Don't you remember the first time I ever called you William?
   William (*moving to the stool* r.). No, and I think I've had enough of this schoolgirl stuff. It's like being forcibly fed with golden syrup. (*He sits.*)
   Helen (*easing* r.c.). You're envious really, y'know.
   William (*horrified*). What—of that—mushy idiocy!
   Philip (*half rising*). Paul! Rosemary! (*He burlesques* Paul *and* Rosemary's *eager, happy looks and tones.*)
   Helen (*coolly*). Not of what he's doing, but of his state of mind. (*She breaks* r. *to* William.) And now you're going to see the next stage. Do you remember what the next stage is?
   William (*cheering up a little*). Yes. Bed.
   Helen (*moving up* r.c.). No. These aren't that kind. (*She turns.*) Think now. (*She sits on the rostrum* r.c.) He's taken her out for several evenings—dining—dancing, to a play or a film—and they're not shy any longer but are beginning to talk.
   William. Yes, I know now. They're beginning to talk their heads off, and everything that each of them says, the other thinks is wonderful. The way they have the same tastes, the very same likes and dislikes—it's miraculous.
   Helen. She'll have to cheat a bit, of course.
   William (*sardonically*). Oh, of course!
   Helen. But not so much as you think.
   William. Look at the way you pretended to like chess and be interested in politics.
   Helen (*scornfully*). Oh!—chess and politics, there's a limit! But she won't have to cheat very much—she's still an impressionable and rather unformed sort of girl, and his very (*she rises and eases* r.) feeling for her, and her response to it, do really bring her unconsciously into line with his point of view.

(*Lights Cue 11. During the following episode,* Helen *exits quietly through the arch* r., *to make her change.*)

B

EPISODE 4

The Curtains open to reveal another corner of the drawing-room in ROSEMARY'S *home.*
  There is an easy chair with cushions R.C., *with a pouffe down* L. *of it.*
  (*See the Ground Plan at the end of the play.*)
  PAUL *is sitting in the chair,* ROSEMARY *on the pouffe. Both are in evening dress, and are very eager, inwardly excited.*

PAUL (*eagerly*). I never knew you'd been there.
ROSEMARY (*eagerly*). Yes, I absolutely loved it. I've always been hoping to go there again.
PAUL. So have I. By Jove, if we could only—— (*He breaks off, pauses a moment, then resumes.*) And the castle, you know, is one of the most amusing pieces of baroque I know.
ROSEMARY. Yes, isn't it ? I adore baroque.
PAUL. Well, I wouldn't go so far as that. It's *amusing*.
ROSEMARY. That's what I meant, Paul. It's terribly *amusing*. That's all, of course. No more than that. Not like—well——
PAUL. Let's say, Perpendicular Gothic or French Renaissance.
ROSEMARY. Of course not. They're absolutely wonderful. I've nearly finished that book you lent me on the French Renaissance. Completely enchanting ! Have you played the Sibelius records yet ?
PAUL (*sitting forward*). Yes—I put them on tonight, just before I came out. You're right, of course. He's head and shoulders above all the rest.
ROSEMARY (*joyfully*). Oh—I'm glad you feel like that about him, Paul.
PAUL. Yes, he gives me just the same feeling you described —sort of—you know, cold and stern yet with a kind of deep warmth inside.
ROSEMARY. That's it exactly. It's absurd saying you don't understand music.
PAUL. And it's absurd saying you don't understand architecture, Rosemary. Some people have a natural good taste, a flair, and you're one of 'em. And I haven't met many.

  (*They exchange a smile and lean to each other.*)

ROSEMARY. Won't you have another whisky and soda ?
PAUL. No, thanks. I must go in a minute.

(*They look at each other and smile. There is a moment's pause.*)

WILLIAM (*the interested spectator*). Well, what about it ? Come on. Everything's all set.

PAUL (*slowly, shyly, looking away from her out front*). It's queer, you know!

ROSEMARY. What is, Paul?

PAUL. The way you go on perhaps for years not meeting anybody who's really your own kind, who likes the same things you like, who can have fun with you or be serious, just as the mood takes you both, until you begin to think you're an odd kind of bird and almost alone in the world.

WILLIAM. Extraordinary how people can imagne they're so different from the crowd. (*He turns to* PHILIP *at the piano* R.) Paul and his odd kind of bird! One of the most commonplace fellows I know! Scores just like him eating biscuits and cheese in every club dining-room!

PHILIP (*pointing to the inner stage and indicating the scene again*). Sh-sh-sh!

PAUL (*shyly*). And then, quite suddenly, you meet somebody.

ROSEMARY (*fervently*). Yes, I know.

PAUL. As we met.

ROSEMARY. Yes. And that's the nicest thing anybody's ever said to me.

PAUL (*holding out his hand*). Rosemary!

ROSEMARY (*holding his hand*). Dear Paul!

(PAUL *draws* ROSEMARY *towards him, and kneeling, she is now in his arms and he kisses her. They are enthusiastic but look awkward. The Curtains close. Lights Cue 12.*)

WILLIAM (*rising and moving* C.). Yes, yes! Yes, yes! They'll be hours now excitedly explaining their uniqueness to each other. (*He eases* L.C.)

JOYCE (*stoutly*). Quite right too!

WILLIAM (*surprised*). Joyce, Joyce! (*He breaks to* R. *of the piano* L.)

JOYCE. Well, that's how they feel, and they're quite right.

WILLIAM. Yes, yes, Joyce. Nobody's blaming them. All very natural and pleasant, only of course we don't want to be in at it. All rather cloying and tedious to the onlooker. (*He looks around.*) Where's Helen?

PHILIP. She went out during that last scene.

WILLIAM (*calling*). Helen! Helen! (*He crosses to the arch up* R.)

HELEN (*calling from off* R.). Shut up, I'm here.

WILLIAM (*turning and moving to up* C. *below the rostrum*). What are you doing there?

HELEN (*calling from off* R.). Turning myself into Paul's mother. They're engaged now and Paul is going to introduce Rosemary to his mother. A big moment.

WILLIAM. Undoubtedly a big moment. And I think Rosemary's father ought to put in an appearance.

HELEN (*calling urgently from off* R.). No, that's not necessary. Now don't be *silly*, darling.

WILLIAM (*with dignity and crossing to the arch* L.). There is nothing silly about it.

(*He exits* L. *Lights Cue 13.*)

EPISODE 5

The Curtains open to reveal a corner of the drawing-room in PAUL'S *home.*

There is a curtained window back C. *A table against the wall* R. *with a bowl of flowers on it. The door is* L. *There is a sofa* C. *with cushions on it.*

(*See the Ground Plan at the end of the play.*)

PAUL, L., *and* ROSEMARY, R., *looking rather anxious, are standing together below the sofa.*

PAUL. But, you dear delightful idiot, what have you to be anxious about? I tell you, she'll adore you. After all, I ought to know, she's my mother.

ROSEMARY. I know, darling. That's just it.

PAUL. The only thing you've got to be afraid of is that very soon, if we're not careful, she'll settle down to tell you what I was like when I was cutting my first teeth or going down with whooping cough.

ROSEMARY. Oh—I don't mind that. In fact, I'd love to know what you were like when you were tiny. That's the point about being in love. You want to know *all* about the other person.

PAUL. I'd hate to know about you at the age of two. I wish mother'd hurry up. Though we were rather early.

ROSEMARY (*nervously*). I think she's here.

(PAUL *gives her a reassuring pat and she gives him a rather desperate quick smile.* HELEN *enters* L., *as* PAUL'S *mother. She is wearing a different dress, a grey wig and spectacles perhaps. She proceeds to give a performance as a solemn matron.*)

HELEN (*moving to* L. *of* PAUL). I'm so sorry—well, Paul! (*She smiles.*)

PAUL. Mother, this is Rosemary.

(HELEN *and* ROSEMARY *smile, but stare hard at each other.*)

HELEN (*with a marked change to effusive ordinary tone*). Well, well, well! So this is Rosemary. (*She shakes her head and smiles at* ROSEMARY.) You've given me a real surprise, my dear. I'd begun to think Paul was a born bachelor. And now—here you are. (*She crosses below* PAUL *to* L. *of* ROSEMARY *and kisses her.*)

ROSEMARY (*shyly*). Yes—and—I'm very, very happy.
HELEN. I'm sure you are. And I know Paul is too.
PAUL. Tremendously happy, Mother.
HELEN (*smiling*). And if he's happy, you may be sure I am, having spoilt him all his life.
ROSEMARY (*smiling*). He doesn't seem very spoilt.
PAUL (*very playfully*). Just you wait! Eh, Mother?
HELEN (*archly*). Yes, indeed. Though I may be able to show Rosemary one or two little tricks—to keep you in order.

(*All three smile at each other, rather fatuously.*)

PHILIP (*across to* JOYCE). Oh, Lord! I hate this dialogue.
JOYCE. I know. Loathsome! But it's about what they'd say.

(WILLIAM *enters breezily* L. *in make-up as before as* ROSEMARY'S *father. He crosses above* PAUL *to* L. *of* HELEN.)

WILLIAM. Well, well, well! Here we are, then.
ROSEMARY (*astounded*). But—Father—what are you doing here?
PAUL. This *is* a surprise, sir.
HELEN (*after glaring at* WILLIAM). *My* surprise this time.
WILLIAM. Yes, yes, quite right. Her surprise. (*He crosses below* HELEN *to* L. *of* ROSEMARY.) Most amusing.
PAUL. Yes—but—how did you . . . ?
WILLIAM (*bluffly, breaking up stage* R.). Oh, your mother'll explain.
HELEN (*after another glare at* WILLIAM). You see, dear, Rosemary's father and I are old friends.
WILLIAM (*bluffly, moving down to* R. *of* ROSEMARY). That's right. Old—old—friends.
HELEN. So I told him over the telephone he'd better come along and give you both a surprise.
WILLIAM (*to* ROSEMARY). And here I am, giving you a surprise. (*To* PAUL.) Well, I expect Rosemary and your mother will have lots to talk about—(*he breaks up* R.) so suppose we leave 'em to it.

(PAUL *breaks up* L.)

Eh?
HELEN. No, no. You men stay here while I take Rosemary with me and get to know her properly. (*She moves to* ROSEMARY *and takes her arm.*) I'm sure you must have a lot to say to each other.

(HELEN *leads* ROSEMARY *to the door* L.)

WILLIAM (*bluffly*). Yes, yes, naturally. Young man marrying my only daughter.

(PAUL *moves to the door* L. *and opens it.*)

HELEN (*turning at the door* L.). Yes, well—have a nice intimate man's talk together. Come along, Rosemary.

(HELEN *and* ROSEMARY *exit* L. PAUL *closes the door, then the two men move the sofa a little down* C. WILLIAM *sits* C. *on the sofa.* PAUL *perches himself for a moment or two on the* L. *arm of the sofa. Both men look stiff and uncomfortable and should be deliberately wooden in attitude and speech.*)

WILLIAM. Humph! All right to smoke?
PAUL (*rising and crossing* R. *above the sofa*). Oh—yes, of course. (*He takes his cigarette-case from his pocket.*) Sorry! (*He moves to* R. *of the sofa and offers his case to* WILLIAM.) Cigarette?
WILLIAM (*taking a cigar-case from his pocket*). No, thanks. Never smoke 'em. Cigar?
PAUL (*taking a cigarette himself*). No, thanks. Can't cope with cigars. Wish I could. (*He lights his cigarette.*)

(WILLIAM *takes a cigar from his case and lights it. Both men look straight in front of them throughout the following dialogue, which should be slow and wooden.*)

WILLIAM. I used to smoke a lot of cigars one time.
PAUL. Did you?
WILLIAM. Yes, I did. Used to get 'em by the thousand direct from Cuba. Wonderful cigars.
PAUL. I'll bet they were. (*He perches himself on the* R. *arm of the sofa.*) Best place for cigars, of course.
WILLIAM. Only place for cigars, really.

(*There is a pause.*)

PAUL. Know much about the South African market, sir?
WILLIAM. No, never touch it. Why?
PAUL. Nothing, really. Just wondered. Client of mine seems to have made a lot out of it, that's all.
WILLIAM. I believe you can. Must be in the know, though. (*He pauses.*) D'you ever go out after wild duck?
PAUL. No. Friend of mine does.
WILLIAM. Does he? (*He pauses.*) What's his name?
PAUL. Sanderson.
WILLIAM. Not old Billy Sanderson, used to be out in Malaya?
PAUL. No, this chap's about my age. In the City. He's very keen on wild duck.

(*There is a pause.*)

WILLIAM. It's a wonderful sport.

(*There is a pause.*)

PAUL. I tried my hand at trout—trout last year.
WILLIAM. Did you? (*He pauses.*) Dry fly?

PAUL. Yes.
WILLIAM. I never could get on with it. Needs too much practice for me.
PAUL. Does really. I wasn't much good.
WILLIAM. No, neither was I.

(*There is another pause, then* HELEN *looking her ordinary self again enters by the arch* L., *and moves to below the rostrum at the* L. *end.*)

HELEN (*scornfully*). A nice intimate man's talk together, eh? Just like two people made out of wood, sitting there grunting at each other! What do you think you're doing?
WILLIAM (*handing his cigar to* PAUL *to hold*). Excuse me a moment, my boy. (*He rises.*)
PAUL (*who doesn't see* HELEN). Certainly. (*He slides on to the sofa and sits woodenly at the* R. *end.*)

(WILLIAM *moves to the edge of the rostrum, steps down and closes with* HELEN. *He takes off his moustache to show that he is now his ordinary self.*)

WILLIAM. What's the matter?
HELEN. Is that your idea of a nice intimate talk between a father and his prospective son-in-law?
WILLIAM. Yes.
HELEN (*indignantly*). But—it's just nothing. Cigars and wild duck!
WILLIAM. A bit impersonal, of course.
HELEN. A bit impersonal.
WILLIAM. You can see the reason, can't you?
HELEN. No, I can't.
WILLIAM. Just shows how insensitive you women are.
HELEN (*aghast*). What?
WILLIAM (*coolly*). Yes, insensitive. We can't get up to your loquacious tricks, pouring out floods of horribly intimate stuff, displaying our underclothes.
HELEN. Who wants you to display your underclothes?
WILLIAM. The fact is, we're shy.
HELEN. But what is there to be shy about?
WILLIAM. This biology we're suddenly caught up in. He's shy because very soon he's going to take my daughter away and share a bedroom with her. And I'm shy because I know he's going to . . .
HELEN. Yes, yes, yes.
WILLIAM. We're the shy sex, you know. Always were. Now I'll get back and finish this off.

(*He puts on his moustache, turns, steps up on to the rostrum and sits on the sofa,* L. *of* PAUL, *who hands him back the cigar. The two men play just in the same manner as before.* HELEN *exits by the arch* L. *to change back into* PAUL'S *mother.*)

PAUL. How do you like this car you're trying?
WILLIAM. Very comfortable, but find her a bit sluggish so far.
PAUL. Engine needs running in, eh?
WILLIAM. Probably. But don't think she's very nippy. (*He pauses.*) You fairly busy now?
PAUL. Yes. We're competing for that big Birmingham job.
WILLIAM. Hope you get it.
PAUL. We stand a fair chance. But that's really my partner's pigeon.
WILLIAM. Yes. I suppose—you'll manage to get away all right after the—(*he pauses*) er—(*he pauses*) wedding?
PAUL. Yes. I've fixed that all right. Hope to manage a month.
WILLIAM. Good! Any idea where you're going?
PAUL. Not quite decided yet. Might motor across France and end up at the Italian lakes.
WILLIAM. Good trip. Sorry I can't be with you. (*He guffaws awkwardly.*)

(*They look at each other.* PAUL *laughs awkwardly.*)

(*Shy and solemn now.*) I know you'll try and make her happy, my boy.
PAUL. It won't be my fault if she isn't, sir.
WILLIAM. No doubt. Won't be hers, though. Happiest little thing you ever saw. Not like some of 'em, always whining and moping. Miss her, y'know, my boy. Miss her like the devil. However, there it is, there it is.

(HELEN, *as* PAUL'S *mother, enters* L. *followed by* ROSEMARY. *They look happy and thick as thieves.* PAUL *and* WILLIAM *rise.* ROSEMARY *eases down* L.)

HELEN (*gaily*). Now you two. (*She moves to above the sofa.*) I know you're having a wonderful talk and telling one another all your secrets. Don't stop. But there are drinks in your room, Paul, and I thought you'd like to go along there.
WILLIAM (*crossing to the door* L.). Good idea.

(WILLIAM *exits* L. *to change back to his ordinary self.*)

PAUL (*crossing below the sofa to* R. *of* ROSEMARY). Yes, rather. How's it going, Rosemary?
ROSEMARY. Grand!
HELEN (*moving to below the sofa*). Passed with honours, didn't you, dear? (*To* PAUL.) Now, off you go.

(PAUL *pats* ROSEMARY'S *hand, turns and exits* L. HELEN *sits on the sofa at the* R. *end,* ROSEMARY *crosses and sits on* HELEN'S

L. *They get into a feminine huddle, very confidential and close, and talking rapidly.*)
Yes, dear. I think you're very wise to take a nice little flat at first.
ROSEMARY. I thought a little flat would be best, at first. Afterwards, of course . . .
HELEN. Afterwards, of course, when you've settled down properly, then perhaps Paul might build you a house about twenty or thirty miles out. (*She looks at* ROSEMARY *and smiles.*) But at first, I know you'll both be happier in some convenient little flat in town. Paul's very fond of the country, of course.
ROSEMARY. I am too. I love the country.
HELEN. I'm sure you do. And of course for young children I think the country's perfect. But you've no need to think about that yet. (*She smiles.*) In the meantime, you're quite right to want a nice little flat. Not a service flat, eh?
ROSEMARY. No, I don't think so.
HELEN. Saves trouble with maids, of course. And cooks.
ROSEMARY. But they're so terribly expensive, aren't they?
HELEN. Most of the ones I know are, but there may be cheaper ones now, though what the food and service will be like I don't know. And Paul's rather fastidious about food, you know. Which reminds me, Rosemary, don't try and make Paul give up his club. I know he's so fond of it.
ROSEMARY. Oh—I wouldn't dream of it. Of course not. He'll want to see other men. But I thought if we had a nice little flat somewhere fairly central . . .

(WILLIAM *enters by the arch* L. *and stands up* L. *watching* HELEN *and* ROSEMARY.)

HELEN. Of course, you're absolutely right. You couldn't do better at first than start with a nice little flat, preferably somewhere fairly central. If you could find a reasonably cheap service flat, of course . . .
WILLIAM. I say!
ROSEMARY. Oh—we'd take it like a shot, if it wasn't too dear. Because after all, it would save trouble with maids and cooks.
WILLIAM. I say!
HELEN. That's the point. As long as the food and service are not too bad. Paul's rather . . .
WILLIAM (*almost in despair*). Look here!
HELEN (*after giving* WILLIAM *a sharp look*). My dear, I'm sure I've kept you too long from Paul. Run along to his room, where I was showing you the photographs, and you'll find him there.
ROSEMARY (*rising spontaneously*). Oh—I'm so happy.

(WILLIAM *turns, moves to the stool* L. *and sits.*)

HELEN (*rising*). I know you are, Rosemary, and I think you've every right to be, for you're a very lucky girl. (*She closes with* ROSEMARY, *smiles and kisses her.*)

(ROSEMARY *turns and exits* L. HELEN *looks at* WILLIAM, *turns to the sofa and pushes it up stage with her foot. The Curtains close. Lights Cue 14.* WILLIAM *rises, mounts the rostrum and with his back to the audience, puts his head through the Curtains and calls to* HELEN.)

WILLIAM (*calling*). I'm sorry—I say—I'm sorry. (*He turns and speaks to* PHILIP.) I believe she's annoyed.
PHILIP. I know she was.
JOYCE. She was furious—and quite right too. You deliberately broke into her scene.
WILLIAM (*breaking off the rostrum and crossing to* L.C.). But she interrupted me when I was Rosemary's father.
JOYCE. Yes, but . . .
WILLIAM (*stamping his foot*). Still, I'll try again. (*He turns, mounts the rostrum again and calls.*) I'm sorry. (*He pauses, then turns.*) Hearing me, of course, but not answering. (*He calls again.*) I'm sorry. (*He pauses, then moves to* R.C. *of the rostrum.*) They don't call that conversation, an exchange of views, opinions, ideas, experiences, do they? They were going round and round in a tiny circle. They were simply making cooing noises at each other.
JOYCE (*rather sharply*). Of course they were. They knew that.
WILLIAM. Well, but what's the point of it?
PHILIP. I've been wondering for years.

(HELEN *enters by the arch* R.)

HELEN (*moving to below* WILLIAM). Don't be so dense. (*She looks up at* WILLIAM *still on the rostrum.*) A girl has just met the mother of the man she's going to marry. A woman has just met the girl her son is going to marry. An ordeal for both of them.
WILLIAM. Yes, I can see that, dense as I am.
HELEN. Well, then they discover, to their great relief, that they're ready to like each other. The ordeal's over. It's going to be all right.
WILLIAM. And so instead of exchanging experiences, opinions, ideas . . .
HELEN. They'll do that much later on.
WILLIAM. They make a lot of nice agreeing noises together, eh?
HELEN. That's it. (*She turns and moves with a funny walk to the stool* R., *demonstrating her next remark.*) Women can't jog along on parallel lines as men seem able to do. (*She sits on the stool* R.) They're always either going away from each other or

coming together. And these two were coming together, and proving it. See?
WILLIAM. Yes, but what a life.
HELEN. Of course, it's ten times harder than being a man. But far more amusing, I fancy. (*She hesitates.*) Now this is rather awkward.
WILLIAM (*breaking off the rostrum and moving to* L. *of* HELEN). Why, what's wrong?
HELEN. We have to be two different characters soon—guests at the wedding reception.
WILLIAM. Oh, have we? That's all right. (*He turns and crosses to* L.C.) I shall be Major Spanner, back from the East and an old friend and admirer of the bride. (*He pauses and breaks up* L.) No trouble about that.

(WILLIAM *turns and exits* L. HELEN *rises and moves* C.)

HELEN. Now, Joyce dear, I think we ought to show Paul and Rosemary just for a minute before the wedding. Something romantic—young—touching.
JOYCE (*rising and moving* L.C.). Yes.
HELEN. A rainy evening in Spring—wet lilac—and the moon lighting her upturned face.
PHILIP (*rising and moving* R.C.). Then you'll want some music.
HELEN. Essential.

(HELEN *turns, moves to the arch* R. *and exits.*)

JOYCE. Chopin, I think.
PHILIP. Certainly. One of the Nocturnes?
JOYCE. No. The *Fantasy Impromptu* middle section.
PHILIP (*turning, moving to the piano* R. *and leaning against it*). All right, but don't go wrong with the Triplets in the left hand.
JOYCE (*moving to* R.C.). No, of course not. Yes, Chopin coming through some mysterious lighted window. Didn't you always think, when we were young, that there was something magical about those houses where somebody was playing a piano?
PHILIP (*easing down* R.). No, I didn't.

(JOYCE *takes a step towards* PHILIP, *who reacts to this and breaks away.*)

JOYCE. You didn't? Why, I used to feel there must be something terribly special about the people in that house—that they were living an enchanted life that I'd never know. What's the matter with you?
PHILIP (*sighing*). I suppose the trouble is I just don't think big, beautiful thoughts. (*He moves to the piano-stool* R.)

JOYCE (*turning and crossing to the piano-stool* L.). Oh, you're hopeless. (*She sits at her piano.*)
PHILIP. Well, I think we're all set. Lights! (*He sits at his piano.*)

(PHILIP *commences to play—Music Cue 7. Lights Cue 15.* PAUL *and* ROSEMARY, *wearing light raincoats and walking close and lovingly, enter by the arch* R. *They stop* C. *where they are illuminated in a moonlight spot.*)

ROSEMARY. Darling!
PAUL. What, darling?
ROSEMARY. The lilac.
PAUL. Yes, marvellous.

(JOYCE *and* PHILIP *commence to play the Chopin music softly.* ROSEMARY *and* PAUL *listen rapturously.*)

ROSEMARY. Chopin. Perfect!
PAUL. Perfect. (*He turns to her.*) Only three days now, darling.
ROSEMARY. Only three days.
PAUL. I love you.
ROSEMARY. I love you.

(PAUL *and* ROSEMARY *kiss, turn and exit together by the arch* L. *The moonlight fades. Lights Cue 16.* JOYCE *and* PHILIP *commence to play a quiet amusing version of the wedding-march, increasing volume as the lights come up. Lights Cue 17.*)

EPISODE 6

The Curtains open to reveal a corner of a large room where the wedding-reception is being held.

There is a long trestle table up C. *covered with a white cloth. On it are glasses, champagne, a wedding-cake, food, etc. There is a chair* L. *of the table, and a palm on a stand in the corner. Two chairs stand against the wall* L. *The entrance is* R.

(*See the Ground Plan at the end of the play.*)

There is a lot of noise off stage, both direct and recorded—chatter, laughter, noise of plates and glasses, etc. HELEN *enters* R. *as Mrs de Folyat, a handsome vivacious widow of about thirty-five with an intense arch manner. She carries a champagne glass which she sets down on the table. She then crosses to the chair down* L. *and sits.* WILLIAM *now enters* R. *as Major George Spanner, a military, rather wooden, bronzed man about forty, who is slightly tight in a rather depressed fashion. He carries a top hat and umbrella.* WILLIAM *moves* C., *and stands a moment busy removing bits of confetti from his clothes.*

HELEN (*shouting*). I beg your pardon.

ACT I]   EVER SINCE PARADISE   25

WILLIAM (*shouting*). Sorry. (*He breaks* L. *to her.*) What did you say?
HELEN (*shouting*). I said " I beg your pardon."
WILLIAM. Certainly—certainly.
HELEN (*shouting*). What time is it?
WILLIAM. Sorry—can't hear you.

HELEN (*rising and shouting at the top of her voice*). I said——

(*The Pianists cease playing suddenly. All noises off cease abruptly at the same moment, so that* HELEN'S *voice sounds very loud indeed across the silence.*)

—(*still shouting at the top of her voice*) what time is it?

(WILLIAM *glances suspiciously at* HELEN.)

WILLIAM (*looking at his watch*). Twenty to four.
HELEN. What a ghastly hour! Let me see, aren't you Major Spanner?
WILLIAM (*at* R.C.). Yes. Sorry—I don't remember.
HELEN (*at* L.C.). No, we weren't introduced. Somebody pointed you out to me. I'm Mrs de Folyat.
WILLIAM. Oh, yes. How d'you do?
HELEN (*waving to somebody off* R.). Do you think it all went off very well?
WILLIAM (*looking up* R., *trying to see to whom* HELEN *is waving*). Suppose so. No judge really. Don't care for all this business. Beastly functions.
HELEN. Definitely. Let me see, you're out East, aren't you?
WILLIAM. Yes. (*He pauses.*) Rubber.
HELEN (*again waving to somebody off* R.). That must be wonderful.
WILLIAM. It was once. But ever since the bottom dropped out of the market, it's been terrible.
HELEN (*with vague enthusiasm*). Yes, but the life there—the colour, the romance, the mystery! The temple bells. The sense of eternity. Do you practise yoga?
WILLIAM (*horrified*). Good Lord! No! (*He takes out his handkerchief, which is filled with confetti that showers over him as he mops his brow.*) I'm not in India, by the way. Straits Settlements. Fifteen hundred miles away from India.
HELEN. Is it really? But then I suppose it's all much bigger out there than one imagines.
WILLIAM. Oh—enormous. People here have not the faintest notion. They ask me to look up fellas who are two thousand miles away from my place.
HELEN (*who is looking vaguely about her*). Do they really? I wonder why? (*She waves, a very big one this time, to somebody presumably leaving, off* R.)

WILLIAM (*disturbed, and looking to where she is waving*). Well, because they don't realize these fellas are two thousand miles away.

HELEN (*confidentially*). I think I shall slip away now. This seems a good chance. (*She moves down* C. *to below the Curtain line.*)

WILLIAM (*with a quick glance round*). Yes, rather. I was just going out. Join you, I think. (*He puts on his top hat and closes with* HELEN *down* C.)

(*The Curtains close behind them. Lights Cue 18. They stand, looking relieved, as if they had sneaked out of an hotel. It is now presumed they are in a street.*)

HELEN (*taking a deep breath*). Ah! It's so good to be in the fresh air again.

WILLIAM. Yes. Frightful row in there. Hate these scrimmages. (*He raises his umbrella and waves it to an imaginary taxi.*) Taxi!

HELEN (*archly*). Are you bride or bridegroom?

(*There is a moment's pause.*)

WILLIAM (*astounded*). What?

HELEN. I mean, one of her friends or one of his?

WILLIAM. Oh, one of hers. Don't know him at all. Known Rosemary since she was a child. Friend of the family. Grown up to be a very fine girl.

HELEN. Has she? (*She waves and calls.*) Taxi!

WILLIAM (*with genuine enthusiasm*). Yes, decidedly. No doubt about that. Weybridge is a very lucky fella. Hope he realizes it.

HELEN. Major Spanner, I do believe . . . (*She breaks off.*)

WILLIAM (*intimidatingly wooden*). What?

HELEN. No, no, I don't know you well enough. I mustn't say it. As a matter of fact I don't know her at all. And I've only recently met Paul Weybridge. He's an architect, you know.

WILLIAM. Yes, so I gather.

HELEN. And a very clever one. He's been adding a little wing to my little place in the country, *quite* brilliantly.

WILLIAM. He has, has he? (*He waves his umbrella again and calls.*) Taxi!

HELEN. I couldn't help thinking it a pity that a man who has, obviously, such a tremendous future should go and——

WILLIAM. What?

HELEN. Now, now, Major Spanner, you mustn't tempt me to be indiscreet.

WILLIAM (*bewildered*). Didn't know I was doing.

HELEN. Besides, it's quite clear I can't expect any sympathy from *you*.

WILLIAM (*stiffly*). Now—look here, Mrs de Folyat, if you're suggesting he oughtn't to have married because his wife isn't good enough for him . . .

HELEN. Now I never *said* that. I merely hinted that perhaps——

WILLIAM. Because if so, I'll give you *my* opinion, as a man who's seen a good deal of the world.

HELEN. And what is your opinion, Major Spanner?

WILLIAM (*stiffly*). That that little girl—Rosemary—is worth ten of him—yes, ten of him. (*He calls and waves his umbrella.*) Taxi! Ah, got it. (*He raises his top hat and is showered with confetti which was concealed in it.*) This one, I think.

(*Lights Cue 19.* HELEN *and* WILLIAM *break off the rostrum and exit by the arch* L. JOYCE *and* PHILIP *begin to play the final theme of the act—Music Cue 8. Lights Cue 20.*)

EPISODE 7

The Curtains open to reveal the balcony of an hotel in Southern Europe.
Back C. *is the bedroom window, French pattern, standing slightly open.*
(*See the Ground Plan at the end of the Play.*)

PAUL L., *wearing a dressing-gown, and* ROSEMARY R., *wearing a wrap, enter through the window and lean on the balcony close together, looking out into what is obviously a wonderful moonlight night. The Pianists play softly before* PAUL *and* ROSEMARY *speak, and continue softly throughout.*)

ROSEMARY. I feel that you and the night are almost one;
I seem as near to you when I stare into the night,
Losing my self in the green ivory world
The moon has carved, as when I felt your heart
Dividing each precious moment with my own!
And when you are so close my eyes have lost you
To my lips, I seem to float in the wide night
And behind my eyelids rises another moon.

(*There is a pause.*)

PAUL. Men are restless and nearly always alone,
Going off in pursuit, nosing along a trail,
Following a rumour of gold to the waterless hills.
Now here comes to an end for me many a trail
That never had a thought in it of women and love.
Now there is nothing I wish to find.

(*He puts his arms round* ROSEMARY.)

ROSEMARY. There should be words that ring out joy like bells,
But I know none. There is sorrow in all words.
PAUL. If my heart still drums it is to stop my ears
Because even tonight from somewhere beyond the moon
Still roars into the abyss the cataract of time.
ROSEMARY. Then take hold of this night and keep it fast
Never, never forget it.
PAUL. I shall not forget.

(*He holds* ROSEMARY *close against him, and she leans her head on his shoulder. Lights Cue 21.* HELEN *enters by the arch* R., *dressed as her normal self, and moves to* R.C.)

HELEN (*in happy excitement*). Now I'm a woman too, and
    not a mere voice,
And blast all supercilious commentary!
Come on, give me that Mediterranean moon,

(*The moonlight spreads full on her too now.*)

And the right man, and I too can kiss
And rave the very stars out of the blue.

(*She calls sharply.*)

William, you idiot! (*Then in soft cajoling tone.*) Oh, Bill, my
    sweet, come on!

(*Lights Cue 22.* WILLIAM *enters by the arch* L. *dressed as his normal self, and moves to* L.C.)

WILLIAM (*in fine form*). And here I am. Hey—spill that
moonshine. Spill it and spread it, boys.

(*The moonlight spreads full on him too now.*)

Ah, that's better. (*He looks across at* HELEN.) God, what a
night! And, Helen—what a girl!
HELEN. You fat, conceited and adorable fool.
You've Paul and Rosemary to thank for this.
WILLIAM (*grandly*). And Adam and Eve and the angel who
sometimes nods, Helen, and lets us slip under his sword at
Eden's gate.

(*There is a pause. Lights Cue 23. The Pianists continue playing through the pauses.*)

PAUL. Rosemary!
ROSEMARY. Paul!

(*There is a pause.*)

JOYCE. Philip!
PHILIP. Joyce!

(*There is a pause. Lights spread to cover* JOYCE *and* PHILIP.)

HELEN. William!
> (*There is a pause.*)

WILLIAM. Helen!

(*The Pianists crash into triumphant music.* PAUL *and* ROSEMARY *are close together.* HELEN *and* WILLIAM *extend their arms to each other.* PHILIP *and* JOYCE *stare happily across as they play. If an orchestra is being used, it can here take up the music of the two pianos.*)

The CURTAIN *falls.*

ACT II

The setting is the same.
  The inner Curtains are closed. Shortly before the CURTAIN *rises,* PHILIP *and* JOYCE *commence playing the introduction at their respective pianos. Music Cue 9.*

When the CURTAIN *rises they are playing fairly briskly. Shortly, however, it begins to flag and suddenly* JOYCE *stops altogether and looks angrily at* PHILIP, *who, after plodding a bar or two by himself, also stops.* JOYCE *rises and crosses to* L. *of the piano* R.

PHILIP. What's the matter?
JOYCE (*angrily*). You know very well what's the matter.
PHILIP. I don't.
JOYCE. Of course you do.
PHILIP (*annoyed*). I tell you I don't. All I know is that you suddenly stopped playing.
JOYCE. And I stopped playing because I couldn't stand it any longer.
PHILIP. Couldn't stand what?
JOYCE. Couldn't stand the sight of you there, obviously with no interest whatever in what we were playing, just bored and not making any effort to hide it. I suppose if it had been Margery Walker you'd been playing with, your eyes would have been half out of your head and you'd have been bouncing all over your piano.
PHILIP (*rising, with an irritating air of patience*). Would you mind telling me what on earth Margery Walker has to do with it?
JOYCE. Oh—don't be so pompous!
PHILIP (*with the same manner as before*). I'm not being pompous. I'm merely asking a reasonable question. What has . . . ?
JOYCE (*furiously*). Oh—shut up! (*She breaks* L.)
PHILIP (*resuming his seat, with injured dignity*). Certainly. Certainly. Only too delighted. (*He begins to whistle the theme of the second overture and taking a newspaper from his pocket very ostentatiously buries himself behind it.*)

(*There is a pause.*)

JOYCE (*turning*). How can you sit there—pretending to read a newspaper!
PHILIP (*turning on his stool, with an irritating air of calm, to face down stage*). I'm not pretending to read. I *am* reading. I notice here, for instance, that a man called Worsnop has just

found on his estate several Roman coins. The coins, it says, were in an excellent state of . . .

JOYCE (*turning and crossing to her stool*). I haven't the least desire to hear anything about your ridiculous coins. (*She sits at her piano.*)

PHILIP. Thank you! (*He resumes reading the newspaper.*)

(JOYCE *glares across at* PHILIP *in angry despair.* WILLIAM, *smoking a pipe and carrying a copy of "The Times", enters by the arch* L. *He looks rather grumpy. He drifts down stage to* L.C. JOYCE *brightens up when she sees him.*)

JOYCE (*rising and leaning across her piano to* WILLIAM). Hello, William.

WILLIAM (*not interested*). Hello!

JOYCE (*with forced brightness*). Any news?

WILLIAM (*opening the paper and moving to his stool* L.). I haven't really looked at the paper yet.

JOYCE. I don't mean in the paper. I mean, have *you* any news?

WILLIAM (*blankly*). Me? Oh—no—nothing at all. (*He sits on the stool* L. *and buries himself behind the newspaper.*)

(JOYCE *stamps her foot, and screams at the men. They both look over their papers at her, then at each other, shake their heads, and resume reading.* JOYCE *sits at her piano and plays several hideously-sounding chords—Music Cue 9a. The men again appear from behind their papers, look at her with silent reproach, then resume reading again.* HELEN *enters briskly and cheerfully by the arch* R., *and crosses to* R. *of* WILLIAM.)

HELEN. William!

WILLIAM (*looking over his paper at* HELEN *without interest*). Yes, my pet? (*He resumes reading.*)

HELEN (*breaking* C. *and speaking rather like a guide-lecturer*). Pay attention. Now, we're going forward several years in the history of Paul and Rosemary. Last time we saw them, you remember, they were on their honeymoon. Five or six years have passed since then. Rosemary has had a baby, now a very nice little boy between three and four, called Robin.

PHILIP (*looking at* HELEN *over his paper*). He doesn't come into this, does he? I mean, you don't show us little Robin bringing his parents together again in the end, do you?

HELEN (*severely*). No, of course not. You see that sort of thing at the films, not here.

PHILIP. Yes, dear, I know, but when you said they now had a nice little boy, I began to be worried.

HELEN. You needn't worry. And by the way, I'm not really talking to you, I'm talking to William.

(PHILIP *resumes reading his paper.*)

WILLIAM (*looking blankly at* HELEN *over his paper*). Yes, my love, I'm listening.
HELEN (*breaking* L. *to* WILLIAM). Move your stool round a bit or you won't see anything.
WILLIAM. Certainly. Certainly. (*He puts his pipe in his pocket, rises, moves his stool a little up stage, sits and resumes reading.*)
HELEN (*moving* C.). So now, after missing these first years of marriage, we now find Paul and Rosemary comfortably settled in London. And here is an average evening. (*She crosses to her stool* R. *and sits.*)

EPISODE 1

The Curtains open to reveal part of the drawing-room of PAUL *and* ROSEMARY'S *home.*

Backstage C. *is a window with a built-in seat. The window-curtains are closed. Against the wall* R. *is an occasional table with a telephone and a box of cigarettes on it. The door is* L. *A small coffee-table stands* C. *with two armchairs, one each* R. *and* L. *of it.*

(*See the Ground Plan at the end of the Play.*)

PAUL, *buried behind a copy of the "Evening Standard", sits* L. ROSEMARY, *fidgeting with a book, sits* R. *Both are rather more mature than when we saw them last.* WILLIAM *and* PHILIP *continue reading their papers and pay no attention whatever to the scene, to the disgust of* HELEN *and* JOYCE. *There is a pause.*

ROSEMARY. I saw Diana Ferguson this morning.
PAUL (*muttering*). Don't know her.
ROSEMARY. Yes, you do know her. She says she's expecting her husband back from India at the end of the month.

(PAUL *merely grunts.*)

(*She looks at him in disgust, then tries again.*) They're taking a house in South Devon for his leave. Then she wants to go back with him this time. And I must say I don't blame her. Do you? (*She pauses, waiting for a reply.*)

(PAUL *does not reply.*)

(*She resumes, keeping her temper with some difficulty.*) Is there anything particularly interesting in that paper, dear?
PAUL (*looking over his paper at her blankly*). What?—no.

(*The Curtains close.*)

HELEN (*rising and crossing to* WILLIAM). William—you're the limit! (*She snatches the paper away from him and breaks to* C.)

Act II] EVER SINCE PARADISE 33

WILLIAM (*rising and closing to* L. *of* HELEN). Now don't be silly, Helen. I'm reading that paper.
HELEN (*crumpling the paper behind her back*). You were, but now you've stopped. I don't believe you noticed Paul and Rosemary at all, did you?
WILLIAM. Well, I'll tell you .
HELEN. Did you?
WILLIAM. No, I didn't.
HELEN. You were too busy staring at that newspaper. What's in it?
WILLIAM. Nothing. Absolutely nothing today. Very dull.
HELEN. I take the trouble to show you Paul and Rosemary having a typical evening . . .
WILLIAM (*warming as he goes along*). Yes, yes, but I don't want to see them. Let's leave them alone. That's what's the matter with the world now. Everybody interfering with everybody else. Everybody wanting to know what everybody else is doing and saying and thinking. Nobody's left alone. Not for a single half-hour is anybody left alone. Well, I say, leave them alone. Refuse to indulge in this universal idiotic and shameless curiosity. Just hand me my paper, will you?
HELEN. Why? It's only crammed with information about other people, news of somebody else's business, all arranged (*she hands the now crumpled paper to* WILLIAM) to satisfy an idiotic and shameless curiosity.

(PHILIP *ceases reading, folds his paper and puts it in his pocket.*)

WILLIAM (*taking the paper from* HELEN *with cold dignity*). It's one thing to acquaint yourself with what's happening in the world—(*he smoothes and folds his paper*) and quite another thing to poke your nose into other people's private affairs. (*He breaks* L.) However, if you won't see it, you won't. (*He changes his tone and closes to* L. *of* HELEN.) Now, I suppose you want me to have a look at this pair of yours, several years after marriage, just to show me how dissatisfied she is. (*He puts his paper in his pocket.*)
HELEN. If you'd seen and heard——
WILLIAM. I saw and heard enough. She's not really dissatisfied with him—although she thinks she is—but she's dissatisfied because she can't have her cake and eat it——
HELEN (*cutting in, vehemently, and breaking* R.). If there's one thing I loathe it's that bit of misery about not being able to have your cake and eat it. (*She leans on the piano* R.)
PHILIP. You all do.
WILLIAM (*easing to* R.C.). Yes. So she'll begin taking her dissatisfaction out of him. And it's not his fault.
HELEN \} (*together*). Of course it is.
JOYCE /

HELEN (*moving to her stool* R.). Just stuck there, with his head in the paper. (*She sits.*)

WILLIAM (*breaking to* C.). But he has to read the paper some time and probably it happens that he's been busy all day.

HELEN. And probably not. But that's not the point. The point is he's beginning to treat her as if she weren't really there. All she wants is a little politeness, a little interest—a——

WILLIAM. I know what she'd like. (*He turns and crosses up* L.) Now I'll show you. (*He claps his hands and calls.*) Scene as before! (*He breaks to his stool* L. *and sits.*)

EPISODE 2

The Curtains open to reveal the same scene.

ROSEMARY *is sitting* R. *eating chocolates*, PAUL *is sitting* L. *reading his paper.*

ROSEMARY. I saw Diana Ferguson this morning.

PAUL (*immediately setting his paper aside*). Did you, darling? When's her husband coming on leave from India?

ROSEMARY. At the end of the month.

PAUL (*brightly astonished*). No!

ROSEMARY. Yes. She's awfully excited.

PAUL. Of course. He must be too. I know I'd be almost off my head with excitement if we'd been separated so long. They ought to take a furnished house somewhere for his leave.

ROSEMARY (*triumphantly*). That's just what they have done. In South Devon.

PAUL. In South Devon? Oh, they ought to have a grand time there. I know *we* should.

(*They lean to each other and smile.*)

ROSEMARY. She wants to go back with him this time. And I must say I don't blame her. Do you?

PAUL. No, I don't. Just imagine if it were us! How lucky we are to be able to be together without either of us making any sacrifices. (*He blows* ROSEMARY *a kiss.*)

ROSEMARY. Yes, darling. (*She smiles across at him.*) But I'm keeping you from your newspaper.

PAUL. Oh, no. (*He throws the newspaper away over his* L. *shoulder.*) I'd much rather have a good talk about *us*, and especially about you. (*He rises, crosses to* ROSEMARY, *bends over and kisses her.*)

WILLIAM (*rising and crossing to* L. *of* HELEN). And that's quite enough of that.

(*The Curtains close.*)

Now, Helen, that's what she'd like—or what she thinks she'd like, and, honestly, what do you think of it?

HELEN. I've always tried to be honest with you, Bill, haven't I?

WILLIAM. Except when we're quarrelling—yes.

HELEN. So, I'll admit that for an ordinary conversation—not a special occasion, mind you, making it up or celebrating an anniversary——

WILLIAM. No, no—an ordinary conversation at the conjugal hearth.

HELEN. —it did strike me as being a wee bit fatuous and sickly.

WILLIAM. Exactly. Like sitting down after dinner and eating two pounds of chocolate creams.

HELEN. Yes—but it isn't the absence of that stuff that is making her feel dissatisfied. What she feels is that he's beginning to be bored with her.

WILLIAM (*breaking to* C.). Now why? A man comes home tired at the end of a hard day, and naturally he wants to take it easy and . . .

HELEN (*rising and crossing below* WILLIAM *to the arch* L.). Yes, yes, we know all about that, and even women can understand it—(*she stops and turns*) seeing that they often have even harder days and aren't allowed to take it easy and sprawl and yawn in everybody's face. But what infuriates a wife is this sort of thing.

(HELEN *turns and exits by the arch* L.)

WILLIAM. What sort of thing?

JOYCE. Watch and you'll see, William.

(WILLIAM *breaks to the piano* R. *and leans against it.*)

EPISODE 3

The Curtains open to reveal the same scene.

ROSEMARY, *fidgeting with a book, sits* R. PAUL, *buried behind a copy of the " Evening Standard ", sits* L.

ROSEMARY. And I must say I don't blame her. Do you? (*She pauses, waiting for a reply.*)

(PAUL *does not reply.*)

(*She resumes, keeping her temper with some difficulty.*) Is there anything particularly interesting in that paper, dear?

PAUL (*looking over his paper at her blankly*). What? No. (*He half stifles a yawn and resumes reading his paper.*)

(*There is a pause.*)

ROSEMARY. Did anything amusing happen at the office today, Paul?

PAUL (*indifferently*). No, can't remember anything.

(ROSEMARY *looks at* PAUL *despairingly but he doesn't even see it. There is another pause, to establish an atmosphere of boredom, then* HELEN, *wearing a coat, enters* L. *briskly, looking very trim and gay.*)

HELEN (*briskly*). Hello, Rosemary! 'Lo, Paul!

(PAUL *rises, moves above* HELEN *and helps her off with her coat, which he places on the window-seat.*)

Just looked in to ask you about Saturday. (*She sits in the armchair* L.)

PAUL (C. *above the coffee-table*). Saturday, by all means, Helen. By the way, a most amusing thing happened at the office this morning.

HELEN. Oh, really?

PAUL. We've got a new client, a Mrs Dowson, who's actually very rich, but looks a queer, shabby old thing. We've also got a new charlady whose name happens to be Mrs Rowston. (*He laughs through the following speech.*) Well, this morning this Mrs Rowston comes in for the first time, and of course the clerk thinks the name she gives is Mrs Dowson, treats her with enormous politeness, can't understand why she keeps mumbling something about cleaning and keeps apologizing abjectly because my partner and I aren't about. (*He laughs.*)

(HELEN *laughs, but not* ROSEMARY.)

HELEN (*clearly forcing her appreciation*). What a priceless thing to happen!

ROSEMARY. It doesn't amuse me very much, somehow. The only difference between the two women was that one had a lot of money and the other hadn't any. And I don't think that's funny.

PAUL (*patting* ROSEMARY'S *left shoulder*). Oh, nonsense, Rosemary. That's taking it altogether too seriously.

HELEN. Did you read that extraordinary case of the woman who had two flats and lived a completely different life in them?

PAUL (*eagerly*). Yes. (*He sits on the left arm of the armchair* R.) I was just reading about it now. Fascinating business! I don't think she was mad though, do you?

HELEN. No. I believe there was a man in it somewhere.

ROSEMARY. Where *is* this woman?

HELEN. In all the papers today.

ROSEMARY (*rising to* R.; *to* PAUL). And——

(PAUL *rises to* C. *above the coffee-table.*)

—you said there wasn't anything interesting in the paper you were reading.

HELEN (*speaking in her ordinary tone, rising, and stepping down from the rostrum*). All right, Rosemary, I think that's enough. (*She moves down* L.C.) You see, that's what I mean. If a man's tired, all right, let him be tired. It's a bit dull for wives, who've been messing about at home all day, if husbands come back in the evening fit for nothing but sprawling and yawning.

(WILLIAM *breaks to the stool* R. *and sits.*)

ROSEMARY (*stepping down from the rostrum and moving down* C.). But we'll make the best of it so long as they *are* genuinely tired, and not simply bored. But you saw what happened. As soon as another woman, an attractive woman, of course, came in, he was up and sparkling, trying to be amusing, ready to show off as hard as he could.

PAUL (*stepping down from the rostrum and moving down* R.C.). I really can't see that just because I show a little ordinary politeness to a friend—a friend of yours as well as mine—you should work yourself up into a jealous fury.

ROSEMARY. I wasn't jealous, and it just shows how stupid you are to imagine I was. I was annoyed because you could take the trouble to entertain Helen when you'd just proved very plainly you couldn't be bothered to entertain me.

WILLIAM (*whistling and beckoning them up to him*). I see the point.

(PAUL *and* ROSEMARY *turn and break to* L. *of* WILLIAM.)

HELEN (*to the audience*). He sees the point. We're getting on. (*She breaks to* L. *of* ROSEMARY.)

WILLIAM (*turning to* PHILIP). But after all, when somebody calls you have to exert yourself a little, for the sake of ordinary social decency.

PHILIP. And I agree.

(*He breaks off because* ROSEMARY *and* HELEN *are shaking their heads.*)

ROSEMARY. I must say, William, I expected something better than that from *you*.

PAUL (*bitterly*). Not from *me*, of course, being only your husband.

WILLIAM (*rising suddenly and breaking down* R.). " A wife ", said Dostoieffsky, after covering himself with glory at a shooting gallery, when his wife had been angry with him for trying to shoot at all. " A wife," he observed profoundly, " is the natural enemy of her husband."

PAUL. And I know exactly what he means.

PHILIP. So do I and I wish I didn't.

HELEN. And I never heard anything more ridiculous. (*She*

turns and crosses to upstage of the piano L.) I'm surprised at you, William.
ROSEMARY (*turning and crossing to* R. *of the piano* L.). So am I. (*She turns and leans against the piano.*)
JOYCE. I thought he was intelligent.
WILLIAM. I am intelligent and so was Dostoieffsky.
ROSEMARY (*bitterly*). The point is, having another woman there, he was no longer bored.
HELEN (*upstage of* ROSEMARY). Perfectly obvious and perfectly maddening.
JOYCE (*rising and easing below the piano*). Haven't we all seen it, over and over again?

(WILLIAM *moves and leans against the piano* R.)

PHILIP (*rising angrily and easing to below the piano*). Because you're so childish. You want everything at once.
PAUL. You can't have it both ways.
WILLIAM. You can't have your cake and eat it.

(*The women all make a slight break forward to* L.C.)

JOYCE		
ROSEMARY	(*together, angrily*).	Oh, stop talking rot! What can't we have both ways?
HELEN		Oh, don't begin about that cake!

(*The men laugh together at this. The women give each other apologetic little smiles, drift back to the piano* L., *group themselves round it and turning, all glare at the men, who make a slight break forward and begin speaking at once.*)

PHILIP		It's perfectly simple and I'll explain.
PAUL	(*together*).	What I mean by not having it both ways is . . .
WILLIAM		Wanting to have your cake and eat it means this . . .

(*The women laugh together at this. The men apologize to each other in a hearty, masculine style, drift back to the piano* R. *and group themselves round it.*)

PHILIP. Sorry, old man! You were going to say——?
PAUL. Not at all, old boy. My fault. Interrupted you both.
WILLIAM. That's all right, my dear fellow. You go ahead.
JOYCE (*in a dry, hard tone*). Lord help us! When you take a good cool look at them, you wonder why you ever bother. They're so damned idiotic. (*She savagely burlesques the men.*) " No, not at all, old man. Go on, old boy." Urr!
PHILIP. One of us had better speak for the lot.
WILLIAM. Good idea! What about you, Paul?

ACT II] EVER SINCE PARADISE 39

PAUL. No, you're the chap, William. Your job, old boy.
WILLIAM (*muttering*). All right, old boy.
HELEN (*coolly*). They're like schoolboys who've been allowed to sit up late and guzzle and swill as much as they liked and so have all gone to seed.
ROSEMARY. They don't even try—as we do—to keep young outside while letting themselves grow older inside.
HELEN. Just overgrown, sagging, ruined schoolboys.
WILLIAM (*moving* C.). Ladies, after we have fallen in love with you we feel that existence would be intolerable if you are not by our sides, so we marry you. What happens then?
ROSEMARY. You take us for granted and we are bored.
WILLIAM. That is how you see it, but not how we see it.
PHILIP. Hear, hear!
PAUL. Hear, hear!
WILLIAM (*breaking to* R., *with a look at* PAUL). You are now associated in our minds with *Home*, with relaxation, with slippered ease, with all the cosy humdrum of domestic life, with lazy chit-chat . . .
JOYCE (*bitterly*). And sprawling and yawning.
WILLIAM (*breaking to* L.C.). If necessary, yes, with sprawling and yawning. With you we feel we need no longer pretend, for we are at home. (*He breaks to his stool* R.) There is something in most women, however, that feels itself defeated by the ease and familiarity of marriage. (*He mounts and stands on the seat of his stool* R. *and assumes the air and deportment of a political speaker.*) It is not that you dislike domesticity, the slippers and dressing-gown atmosphere. But at any moment when you feel so inclined you think you are entitled to be regarded as a person clean outside this atmosphere, a strange, exciting creature, a figure of romance.
ROSEMARY (*breaking* L.C. *and pointing to* WILLIAM). But that's the point. We *are* strange, exciting creatures, and what's wrong with you men is that you stop thinking we are, and then you diminish us.

(PHILIP *looks at* WILLIAM *and whispers to him.* WILLIAM *bends down and whispers to* PAUL.)

We grow angry because there is a light in us and you will no longer let it shine for you. (*She backs away to the piano* L.)
PAUL (*breaking to* R.C.). But the light has been turned into the domestic lamp and firelight. Your trouble is you want to be courted as well as married. (*He returns to lean on the piano* R.)
HELEN. And why not?
WILLIAM. Because—and this is one of the cakes you can't both have and eat—to our way of thinking one relationship cancels out the other. Husbands take wives for granted, of course they do. They married them in order to take them for granted.

But wives take husbands for granted just as much, and that, ladies and gentlemen, is our case.

(PHILIP *takes* WILLIAM'S *right arm*, PAUL *his left, and* WILLIAM *steps down from the stool.* PHILIP *and* PAUL *shake* WILLIAM *by the hand. The men go into a huddle round the piano* R. PAUL *up stage*, WILLIAM, L., *with his back to the women, and* PHILIP *down stage. The women do likewise round the piano* L., HELEN *up stage*, ROSEMARY, R., *with her back to the men, and* JOYCE *down stage. After a few moments*, ROSEMARY *turns and breaks* L.C.)

ROSEMARY. It doesn't *suit* women to be taken for granted. (*She stamps her foot.*) It withers them. (*She turns her back to the men and returns to* R. *of the piano.*)

(*The men turn and look at the women.* JOYCE *moves to her stool, seats herself at the piano and plays a few mournful chords—Music Cue 10, then pauses a moment.*)

HELEN. What's that?
JOYCE. It's the beginning of a lament for women. (*She resumes playing, and continues to do so softly throughout the women's speeches.*)

(*Lights Cue 1. After a look at each other, the men turn their backs on the scene.*)

HELEN (*breaking to* R. *of* ROSEMARY). Who was the last to enter the Paradise of Eden—and the first out? Woman.
ROSEMARY. The fool who can light up at a single kind word, and bleed at a glance.
JOYCE. Who buys a new hat and hopes against hope.
HELEN (*in a grander style, turning, moving up* C. *and mounting the rostrum*). I sing—after the manner of Walt Whitman, who, nevertheless, has always seemed to me an insufferable old bore—I chant the theme Woman. Not Woman and the joys of the open road, for no woman ever had an open road. All roads are narrow, dark, bristling and dangerous to a woman. Not Woman and the happiness of loafing, hanging about, watching other people work and producing nothing but noble platitudes, because no woman is allowed—by herself or by anybody else—to indulge in such idle antics. Some men are handsomely paid and kept in comfort to prove and preach that the ultimate force in the universe is nothing but Love, and they may or may not believe it. But all women, even the stupidest and ugliest that nobody cares about, act as if this were true. (*She steps down from the rostrum, crosses to the piano* L. *and leans against it.*) And much good it does them.
ROSEMARY (*breaking to* L.C.). It is terrible to be a woman and know in your heart how dependent you are upon other

people, how you wait and wait for some fool of a man, who doesn't happen to have anything better to do, to bring you completely to life.

JOYCE. There are too many of us, that's the trouble.

ROSEMARY. A hurried, indifferent kiss, a hint of a yawn, from some man who isn't really very different from millions of other men, and ice is packed round your heart. (*She returns to* R. *of the piano* L.)

JOYCE. What we need is ice packed round our heads.

HELEN. After being a woman, to be a man must be like having a long rest, a sort of convalescence.

(PHILIP *slides on to his piano-stool and plays some loud, sharp chords—Music Cue 11, which interrupt* JOYCE, *who stops playing. The women all look across at him.* PHILIP *pauses a moment in his playing.*)

PHILIP. Convalescence! You can't imagine what it's like being a man. It's like this. (*He plays some loud, restless, strident music on the piano again.*) I tell you—it's hell. (*He commences playing again, softly now, but with loud chords between speeches.*)

WILLIAM (*breaking to* R.C.). In the fields you see the cows staring at nothing with their great soft eyes, placidly grazing and chewing, cosily manufacturing tomorrow's milk. Look further, into lonely field or dark shed, and you will hear unhappy snorts and grunts and see a majestic but restless form, a creature passionate and bewildered, with a ring through his nose. (*He pauses.*) The bull! And that is Man. (*He moves* R. *to the piano.*)

PAUL (*crossing quickly up* C. *and mounting the rostrum*). Man, fixed for ever in his terrible dualism, the war between the spirit and the senses that no woman can understand. Man, who grasps at the moon, and finds himself eating green cheese. Man, who cannot be lulled by the rhythms of the fat earth and who is haunted by the Paradise you hardly remember. (*He breaks off the rostrum and crosses to the upstage of the piano* R.)

PHILIP (*ceasing to play and speaking sadly*). After all, it is better to buy a hat and hope a bit than to buy dozens of drinks and know there is no hope.

WILLIAM (*moving* C. *below the rostrum, and assuming the air and deportment of a solicitor, presenting his case*). When a pair of lovers declare themselves, one of them thinks he is juggling with the sun, moon and stars, while the other is busy working out how much it will cost to keep a housemaid in one of those nice new bungalows along Elm Avenue.

(*The women do not pay any attention to* WILLIAM. HELEN *is in dumb play with* ROSEMARY *about her stockings.* JOYCE *rises, closes with them and joins in comparing her stockings with the other two.*)

It is safe to prophesy which of these two will come a cropper first. The chaps who saw themselves keeping the sun, moon and stars going, are bound to come down with a bump. The ladies—God bless them—have never left the ground.

PAUL (*crossing quickly up* C. *and mounting the rostrum*). Man—alternating between Don Quixote and Don Juan . . .

(PHILIP *attracts* WILLIAM'S *attention and indicates that the women are not listening.*)

WILLIAM (*breaking up* C. *and speaking to* PAUL). I don't think they're listening, my dear fellow. Better get back on the job. (*He indicates the inner stage.*)

(*Lights Cue 2.*)

PAUL. What? Oh, yes, certainly. (*He moves and sits on the* L. *arm of the armchair* R.)

WILLIAM (*crossing to* HELEN *and* ROSEMARY). Come along, you two. Never should have stepped out of the scene like that, y'know. Spoils the illusion.

(HELEN *and* ROSEMARY *cross and mount the rostrum.*)

HELEN (*to* ROSEMARY *as they cross*). I'll just say good-bye to you both, and then you show how annoyed you are with him, and we'll carry on from there. (*She sits in the armchair* L.)

(ROSEMARY *stands* R. *of the armchair* R. WILLIAM *breaks to his stool* L. *and sits.* JOYCE *sits at her piano* L.)

Well, I must run along, children. Oh what about Saturday? (*She rises.*)

(PAUL *moves to the window-seat, gets* HELEN'S *coat and helps her on with it.*)

ROSEMARY (*coldly*). Paul can go if he likes—but I'm sorry, I can't.

PAUL. But you said . . .

ROSEMARY. I promised to spend the afternoon with father. You go. I'm sure you'll find it very amusing.

HELEN. Settle it between you and give me a ring, one of you, in the morning. 'Bye, darling.

ROSEMARY. Good-bye, Helen.

PAUL. I'll see you out.

(HELEN *and* PAUL *exit* L. ROSEMARY *now looks furious. She picks up her book, hurls it down again into the armchair* R., *crosses and sits in the armchair* L.)

ROSEMARY (*muttering angrily*). Oh, damn—damn—damn!

(PAUL *enters* L., *crosses behind her to the table* R., *picks up the cigarette-box and offers it to* ROSEMARY.)

PAUL (*with forced cheerfulness*). Cigarette, darling?
ROSEMARY (*very cold and distant*). No, thank you.
PAUL (*replacing the cigarette-box on the table* R.). Anything the matter?
ROSEMARY. No, why should there be?
PAUL. I dunno—I just wondered. I thought you were very keen on going with them on Saturday.
ROSEMARY (*miles away*). Did you?
PAUL. Well, you said you were.
ROSEMARY. I haven't the least desire to go with them. I loathe the Sunderlands anyhow. I've always thought your friend Helen had a very queer taste in people.
PAUL (*raising his eyebrows*). My friend Helen now, eh?

(ROSEMARY *does not reply*.)

She used to be your friend too. In fact, you knew her before I did.
ROSEMARY. I only knew her through William. And I *adore* William. I don't dislike Helen, but I think she has some very queer friends and I'd just as soon she didn't bounce in and out like that, even if you have to make such a fuss of her.
PAUL (*very innocently, and sitting in the armchair* R.). Fuss of her! What fuss did I make of her?
ROSEMARY. If you join them on Saturday, you'll be able to have a whole day of it, with funny stories about charwomen and women who live in two flats at once and everything.
PAUL. Look here, I didn't care tuppence about Saturday, but if you insist upon taking that tone about it, all right, I *am* going.
ROSEMARY (*rising*). I should. (*She breaks up* C.) It'll be a nice change for you after being bored at home.
PAUL (*rising angrily*). Now when have I ever said I was bored at home?
ROSEMARY. You didn't need to *say* anything.
PAUL. Well, what have I done then? What's the matter?
ROSEMARY (*stormily, nearly in tears*). Nothing. Everything.

(*She crosses quickly to the door* L. *and exits, slamming the door. The Curtains close.* HELEN *enters by the arch* R., *moves to the piano* R. *and leans against it*.)

HELEN. Well, there they are then.
WILLIAM (*rising and moving to* L.C.). Yes, and I was working out their future. I see three stages waiting for them. First, a stage of constant and bitter quarrelling. Secondly, a stage in which each seeks satisfaction elsewhere. Thirdly, a stage of final separation or a real reconciliation and the beginning of a decent adult life together.
HELEN (*breaking* C. *below the rostrum*). Very good, darling. I couldn't have done it better myself.

WILLIAM. You couldn't have done it as well as I did. (*He breaks* L.)

HELEN. Yes, I could. (*She eases down* C.) Actually, you've left out a stage. You see, with some couples like Paul and Rosemary there's another stage that comes before the constant quarrelling; in this period each partner finds a friend of the same sex that the other partner very much dislikes. It might be called the Unwise Friendship stage.

WILLIAM (*breaking down* L.). You're right. (*He turns to the audience.*) She *is* right, y'know. Very clever woman. Most men, and especially Englishmen, dislike clever women, but I like 'em. So long as they're reasonably good-tempered, of course. (*He pauses.*) An *amiable* clever woman is an absolute treasure. (*He breaks* R. *to* HELEN, *takes her by the hand and leads her down* C.) Thank you. (*He releases* HELEN'S *hand.*)

(HELEN *turns and moves down* R.)

(*To the audience.*) You've probably been wondering what our relationship is—haven't you ? It's very interesting. And perhaps later on—well, we'll see. (*He turns to* HELEN.) You're dead right of course. (*He breaks* L.)

HELEN. Rosemary will suddenly become friendly with some terrible woman whom Paul can't stand.

WILLIAM. And Paul will pick up a pal who's poison to Rosemary.

HELEN. It seems accidental—and yet—I don't know.

WILLIAM. The subconscious does it, I think. It deliberately singles out the type that the other partner loathes. (*He pauses.*) Well, it's up to us, I suppose.

HELEN (*breaking to* C.). Certainly. What are you going to be ?

WILLIAM (*moving* C. *to* L. *of* HELEN). I shall be one of those self-made City bachelors. They're always dining in very expensive restaurants and they put up the money for bad musical comedies. Wives hate them, because they imagine that these fellows have flats somewhere crowded with showgirls drinking champagne-cocktails and playing strip poker.

HELEN (*interested*). And have they ?

WILLIAM. No, it's all an illusion. Nevertheless, the instinct of the wives is right, because these chaps are fundamentally anti-domestic and try to turn the husbands back into bachelors. That's me then. And you ?

HELEN. I shall be Mrs Ambergate—Gloria Ambergate. I'm separated from my husband—he probably cleared out with his typist—and now I've got a down on all husbands and am very, very sorry for the poor wives. And she's gone in for New Thought and Higher Thought and Astral Planes and Auras and Vibrations and she sees everybody's personality in terms of

colour. And she has a general deep soulfulness from which the coarse scoffing male is excluded.
WILLIAM. I know the type. But Rosemary would never put up with her.
HELEN. Oh, yes—she would—for the time. Just because she was sorry for her. It often happens among women. Being members of the gentler and more sympathetic sex . . .
WILLIAM (*astonished*). Members of the *what*?
HELEN (*shouting across to* WILLIAM). The gentler and more sympathetic sex   idiot.
WILLIAM (*breaking up* L.). Yes, I see. Well, that's us then.
HELEN (*to* PHILIP *and* JOYCE). And you two ought to find Leitmotivs for . . .
WILLIAM (*calling across to* PHILIP). Jimmy Mowbray.

(WILLIAM *breaks to the arch* L. *and exits.*)

HELEN (*calling across to* JOYCE). Gloria Ambergate.

(HELEN *breaks to the arch* R. *and exits.*)

PHILIP (*to* JOYCE). Oh, I've got mine. (*He pauses a moment.*) This is Jimmy Mowbray. (*He plays a few notes of cheerful, rather vulgar dance music—Music Cue 12.*)
JOYCE (*to* PHILIP). And this is Gloria Ambergate. (*She plays a snatch of cheaply soulful music.*)
PHILIP. Good. Now we can make 'em into something. (*He rises and announces to the audience.*) Short prelude illustrating this stage of Unwise Friendships. (*He sits again at his piano.*)
JOYCE (*rising and announcing to the audience*). Alternative titles : " What on Earth Do You See in Him—Or Her ? " (*She sits again at her piano.*)

(PHILIP *and* JOYCE *play the prelude. When they have finished, they rise for a moment and bow to each other.*)

EPISODE 4

The Curtains open to reveal the same scene.

PAUL *enters* L. *carrying a tray on which are three glasses and a cocktail-shaker. He crosses to the table* R., *sets down the tray, pours himself a drink and tastes it. He then puts his glass down, picks up the cocktail-shaker and shakes it. As he does so, the telephone bell rings. He puts down the shaker and lifts the telephone receiver.*

PAUL (*speaking into the telephone*). Hello ! . . . Yes . . . (*He laughs.*) Of course it's not too early. Come along at once . . . All right then . . . Good-bye for now. (*He replaces the receiver.*)

D

(ROSEMARY, *carrying a book, enters* L., *moves to the armchair* L. *and sits.*)

Will you have—er—have a cocktail?

ROSEMARY. No, thank you. You know I hardly ever have a cocktail. I think it's an awful waste making them. And why *three* glasses? (*She opens her book.*)

PAUL (*uncomfortably*). Well—as a matter of fact—Jimmy Mowbray rang up to say he might look in.

ROSEMARY (*disgusted*). What again? He'd better come and live here, hadn't he?

PAUL (*with great dignity*). Mowbray happens to be a client of mine.

ROSEMARY. That has nothing to do with it, and you know it hasn't. And what you can see in him I can't imagine.

PAUL. Oh—he's not a bad fellow.

ROSEMARY. He's terrible. And Gloria Ambergate says he has a flat, crowded with chorus girls, all drinking champagne-cocktails. (*She rises and breaks down* L.) Really, Paul, I thought you had better taste than that.

PAUL (*irritably, and moving down* R.). Oh—don't be so snobbish. Jimmy Mowbray may not be your type . . .

ROSEMARY. My type! He's not anybody's type outside a race-course, and non-stop variety. He's . . .

PAUL (*cutting in sharply and breaking to* C.). Jimmy Mowbray's quite a decent, amusing sort of fellow—who might turn out to be a very good client.

ROSEMARY. And then again might not. I wouldn't trust a man like that a yard. Still, I suppose if he wants to turn this house into his cocktail bar, I mustn't complain.

PAUL (*unpleasantly*). Oh—you couldn't complain. You wouldn't know how to.

ROSEMARY (*crossing sharply, above the chairs, to the table* R.). Thank you! (*She lifts the telephone receiver and dials.*)

(PAUL *crosses to the armchair* L., *picks up a paper from the coffee-table* C. *and begins to read.*)

(*She pauses, waiting for the reply, then speaks into the telephone with marked sweetness.*) Oh—is that you, Gloria? . . . Rosemary . . .

(PAUL *looks up and snorts.*)

No, Gloria, you come here . . .

(PAUL *throws the paper down on the table* C.)

Yes, as soon as you like . . . Good. (*She replaces the receiver.*)

PAUL (*glaring at her*). Was that your dear friend, Gloria Ambergate?

ACT II]   EVER SINCE PARADISE   47

ROSEMARY (*moving to* C. *above the coffee-table*). Yes. She's coming across to spend the evening here.
PAUL (*angrily*). If that awful woman comes here I'm going straight out.
ROSEMARY (*with a mock innocent air*). I thought you were probably going out anyhow, with your nice friend, Mr Mowbray. Weren't you?
PAUL (*rather confusedly*). He suggested our dining somewhere —but I hadn't said definitely I would.
ROSEMARY (*in the same tone as before*). Well, now you can, and that'll be very nice for you.
PAUL. I warned you before. If you must see that frightful half-baked woman—and what on earth you can see in her beats me—please don't ask her here when I'm about. I *loathe* the woman. Really, I'm surprised at you, Rosemary. A year or two ago, you couldn't have spent an hour with a woman like that, and now . . .
ROSEMARY (*vehemently*). Yes, *now*—when I have to watch you being dragged off every other night by that—that . . .

(*There is a sharp ring of a bell, off stage.* PAUL *rises, and exits* L.
ROSEMARY *glares after him a moment, moves to the table* R., *picks up the cocktail-shaker, smells its contents and hastily puts it down with disgust. She then moves to the armchair* L. *and sits in it, assuming an air of distant dignity.* WILLIAM, *as Mowbray, enters* L., *followed by* PAUL, *who crosses to the table* R. *and pours out the cocktails.* WILLIAM *stands* C. *above the coffee-table.*)

WILLIAM (*in a brisk staccato tone*). Ah! Good evening, Mrs Weybridge.
ROSEMARY (*coldly*). Good evening.
WILLIAM. Wondered if I might snatch your husband—dine with me to meet another friend just back from South America— just the kind of bloke to amuse Paul. Quiet bachelor evening. Steak and a decent bottle o' wine, y'know—an' perhaps finish our cigars at a variety show.
PAUL. Cocktails? Rosemary?
ROSEMARY (*distantly*). No, thank you.
PAUL (*handing a glass to* WILLIAM). Mowbray?
WILLIAM (*taking the glass*). Ta! Well, down the hatch! (*He drinks, emptying his glass.*)

(PAUL *drinks a cocktail himself.*)

PAUL. Dry enough for you?
WILLIAM. Oh—yes. Do with a dash p'r'aps. Like a dash myself.
PAUL. Ah—sorry about that. (*He turns to the table* R. *and puts down his glass.*)
ROSEMARY (*distantly*). And what is a dash?

WILLIAM (*surprised*). Dash? Don't you know what a dash is? Where have you been? It's absinthe.
ROSEMARY (*condemning it*). Oh, absinthe.
WILLIAM (*not noticing her attitude*). That's it. Absinthe makes the heart grow fonder, eh? (*He guffaws.*) Well, I won't say no to another, old boy. (*He hands his glass to* PAUL.)

(PAUL *pours out another cocktail.*)

Had a hard day today. Market's all over the place. Still, never say die. (*He gives* ROSEMARY *a hearty pat on the back.*) Met a bloke at lunch today who's bringin' that musical show over from New York—and blow the expense.

(PAUL *offers him the drink.*)

(*He takes the glass.*) Y'know, the big smash hit there—*Got What It Takes* or something. (*He breaks* R. *to* PAUL.) Says if he can sneak most of it past the Lord Chamberlain it'll make London's hair stand on end. He's importing all the original girls. (*He nudges* PAUL *with his right elbow.*)
ROSEMARY (*coldly*). I would have thought we'd enough chorus girls here without bringing some all the way from New York.
WILLIAM. That's just your innocence, Mrs Weybridge. These American kids have got something. Ask your husband. Well, down the hatch. (*He drinks.*)

(*There is a sharp ring of a bell, off stage.* PAUL *makes as if to go, but* ROSEMARY *rises and exits* L.)

PAUL (*lowering his voice*). We'd better push off in a minute, Jimmy. This woman's terrible.
WILLIAM. What woman?
PAUL (*grimly*). You'll see.
WILLIAM. Isn't time for it now, but remind me when we get out to tell you the story of the widow and the piano tuner. It'll kill you. (*He laughs, finishes his drink and hands the empty glass to* PAUL.) By the way, this bloke you're going to meet—like most of these lads just back from the pampas or whatever they are—is a bit hot and might want to start a pretty thick sort of evening.

(PAUL *pours out two more cocktails.*)

Have to sit on his head a bit. You don't want any young female society tonight, do you?
PAUL (*offering* WILLIAM *the glass*). No, certainly not.
WILLIAM (*taking the glass*). Same here. Last week-end was bad enough and I've a business to look after. Well, a quick one for the road, eh?

(*They both drink, emptying their glasses.* WILLIAM *hands his empty glass to* PAUL. *They ease to the table* R. PAUL *pours out*

ACT II]   EVER SINCE PARADISE   49

three cocktails. HELEN, *as Gloria Ambergate, enters* L., *followed by* ROSEMARY. HELEN *contrives to register her disapproval of the two men and the cocktails at once.*)
PAUL. Oh—good evening, Mrs Ambergate.
HELEN (*below the armchair* L.). How d'you do?
ROSEMARY (*down* L.). Gloria—this is Mr Mowbray.
WILLIAM. How d'you do? (*He takes his refilled glass from* PAUL.)
HELEN (*coldly*). Good evening.
PAUL (*offering* HELEN *a glass*). Cocktail, Mrs Ambergate? (*He puts the glass on the coffee-table* C.)
HELEN (*sitting in the armchair* L.). Oh—no, thank you. I can't take alcohol in any form.
WILLIAM. Can't you? It's about the only thing I can take nowadays. (*He laughs and looks at his watch.*) Well, Weybridge, better push off, eh? (*He finishes his drink and hands the glass to* PAUL.)
PAUL. I'm ready. (*He finishes his drink and puts both glasses on the table* R.)
WILLIAM. Good night, Mrs Weybridge. (*He picks up the cocktail from the coffee-table* C.) Well, the—skin off your nose! (*He finishes the drink and hands the glass to* PAUL.) Good night, Mrs—— . . . (*He crosses to the door* L.)

(PAUL *puts the glass on the table* R. WILLIAM *exits* L.)

ROSEMARY. Don't be too late, Paul.
PAUL (*crossing to the door* L.). No, I won't be. 'Night, Mrs Ambergate.

(*He exits* L. *closing the door after him.*)

HELEN. That man, Rosemary—who is he?
ROSEMARY (*crossing and sitting in the armchair* R.). He's a client of Paul's. You can say what you like about him. I loathe him.
HELEN. I'm so glad, dear. I was sure you must. He's a dreadfully undeveloped type. *Earthy*—quite earthy. With a kind of muddy brown aura. I wish you could have been at our lecture last Wednesday. Mme Rubbishky gave us a *wonderful* talk on—(*she sits upright in her chair*) I AM THE GREAT ALL.
ROSEMARY. On what?
HELEN (*solemnly*). I AM THE GREAT ALL. And so *profound*—so *stimulating* and yet at the same time so essentially *simple*. We are all of us the Great All. And the Great All is all of us. The whole *thing* was there.
ROSEMARY. I'm not sure I believe in all this, you know.
HELEN. I didn't expect you would, dear, not yet. Perception comes with suffering and loneliness of spirit. You'll see.

Rosemary (*dismayed*). But I don't want any suffering and loneliness of spirit.
Helen. It won't be so bad for you, dear, as it was for me. You'll have friends—certainly *one* friend, darling—who can help and guide. As soon as I saw that man here tonight, and saw him taking your husband away, I knew at once that soon you'll need a friend very badly. (*She lowers her head and body to the* L.) I could *feel* a downward, earthward influence.
Rosemary. But what kind of influence is that, Gloria?
Helen (*swinging her head up and round to* Rosemary). It's downward—earthward, dear—pulling down. I've always been able to feel it, even before I knew what it meant. Chiefly among men, of course. And I've always *known* it was antagonistic. But I myself rejected the influence. I said—(*she rises and stretches her arms above her head*) "You cannot pull me down." (*She drops her arms, and sits again.*)
Philip. I say, Helen, is there much more of this horrible stuff?
Helen (*in her ordinary tones*). Yes, Philip. Hours and hours.
Philip. Then let's cut to midnight. (*He calls.*) Lights!

(*The* Lights *dim to Black-Out, to denote the passage of time—Lights Cue 3.* Philip *plays a chime on his piano—Music Cue 12a.*

The Lights *come up again to full---Lights Cue 4.* Rosemary *has slumped down in her chair, half asleep.* Helen *is discovered lying on the floor* L., *with her head on the chair* L.)

Helen. Good gracious—twelve o'clock already. We've had such a wonderful, lovely satisfying talk, it's just given the evening great golden wings—and—pouf—it's just flown away.
Rosemary (*rising and stifling a yawn*). Yes, hasn't it. (*She helps* Helen *to rise.*)
Helen (*solemnly*). But I do hope nothing has happened to your husband, dear, he's very late.
Rosemary (*crossing below* Helen *to the door* L.). Of course not. Why should it? Just a moment, I'll put the light on.

(*She exits* L.)

Helen (*reflectively*). It's all very well saying "Of course not", my dear. But I can't forget the night I was sitting up late with poor Mildred Fothergill. We heard the ambulance ringing right outside her window, and the telephone went and a voice said, "Come at once, Mrs Fothergill." But of course it was all over by the time she got to the hospital. Mr Fothergill had departed for the Astral Sphere, and had not even insured himself properly.

(*She turns, and exits* L. *The* Lights *dim to Black-Out to denote*

a further passage of time—Lights Cue 5. PHILIP *plays a chime on his piano—Music Cue 12b.*
   The LIGHTS *come up again to full—Lights Cue 6.* ROSEMARY, *now wearing a dressing gown, enters* L. *She crosses to the window back* C. *and looks out. She seems agitated, crosses to the table* R., *and is about to pick up the telephone receiver, but decides not to, and moves to below the armchair* L. *As she is about to sit, the telephone rings urgently. She crosses quickly to the table* R. *and lifts the receiver.*)
   ROSEMARY (*speaking into the telephone*). Yes, yes? . . . (*Then, sharply.*) No, we're not . . Well, I ought to know whether we're the gasworks or not. You've got the wrong number, that's all. (*She replaces the receiver. Muttering.*) Silly idiot!

(*There is the sound of an ambulance bell ringing furiously outside the window. This seems to disturb* ROSEMARY, *and she moves restlessly about the stage* C. WILLIAM *enters by the arch* L. *and moves* L.C.)

   WILLIAM (*breaking to his stool* L.). What's the matter with her? (*He sits.*)
   JOYCE. Paul's late, so now her imagination will get to work. We all do it.

(ROSEMARY *breaks to* C. *below the coffee-table. The* LIGHTS *fade until only a single pink spot illuminates* ROSEMARY. *Lights Cue 7.*)

   ROSEMARY. The hospital, please, driver—and hurry—it's terribly urgent. Yes, nurse, I'm Mrs Weybridge, take me to him. Oh! yes, I'll be brave—I will be brave. (*In a worrying tone.*) I'd have to ask Father to come up to look after things and I couldn't let Robin stay here—perhaps he and Nannie could go to Alice's for the week—and as soon as I'd got them off I'd have to order my black—and then when it was all over I couldn't afford to stay on here—I'd have to sell this house—then try to find a little cottage in the country—and then Robin would have to go away to school—but we'd share our little cottage during all his holidays. (*She sighs very dreamily.*) Yes, dear, it's years and years ago now, and they realize that my Paul was a great architect—and they want me to unveil a memorial to him—it will be a beautiful——

   (*The* LIGHTS *come slowly up to full again. Lights Cue 8.*)

—experience, but, of course, sad too. (*She turns, moves to the armchair* R. *and sits, dabbing her eyes with her handkerchief.*)

(*We now hear* PAUL *off stage, whistling the Mowbray theme, but* ROSEMARY *does not.* PAUL *enters* L. *and moves to* L. *of the armchair* L.)

(*Rising with joy and surprise.*) Paul!

PAUL. I'm sorry, my dear. You shouldn't have waited up.

ROSEMARY (*crossing to him; severely*). Where have you been?

WILLIAM. The eternal question.

(*There is a pause.*)

And now I understand why they always put it so angrily.

PAUL (*crossing above the chairs, to the table* R.). Mowbray took me to his club—and we began playing snooker—and then I couldn't get a taxi. You know how it is, my dear. What have you been doing?

ROSEMARY. Listening to Gloria for hours and hours.

PAUL (*laughing to himself*). Oh! Bad luck.

WILLIAM (*turning to* JOYCE). I wonder if the chump realizes this is his chance. He's had as much as he wants of Jimmy Mowbray, and she's had far more of Gloria Ambergate. I wonder if he realizes this. Oh dear, it doesn't look as if he does.

(*While* WILLIAM *speaks,* PAUL *pours himself out a glass of whisky, but the bottle only contains sufficient for one glass, so he has tipped the bottle up and drained it.*)

PAUL (*drinking*). You know very well, Rosemary, that's a terribly dreary woman.

ROSEMARY. I know—but I'm sorry for her, though I admit she can be an awful bore. But she's lonely. Not like your friend Jimmy Mowbray, who's so pleased with himself.

PAUL (*easing* C. *above the coffee-table*). Well, I'll admit that Jimmy is a bit much at times. But that Oria Glambergate—is a tearily—dreary . . .

ROSEMARY (*crossing to the armchair* L.). Paul—I believe you're tight. (*She sits.*)

PAUL (*swaying about and toying with his glass*). If I say I am, you'll believe I'm not, which wouldn't be quite true. But if I say I'm not, then you'll think I'm very tight, which would be quite wrong. Better ignore the whole thing.

WILLIAM. Now, what's her reaction going to be? She might burst into tears. She might lose her temper and throw something at him. She might rise haughtily and sweep out of the room. Or she . . .

(ROSEMARY *suddenly bursts out laughing. It is quite warm and friendly laughter.* PAUL *seems to her at this moment very funny.*)

JOYCE (*to* WILLIAM, *as* ROSEMARY'S *laughter dies down*). This is his chance.

WILLIAM. Of course it is. He's only to drop down and put his arms round her and babble any nonsense and she's his again.

JOYCE (*scornfully*). But he isn't going to. (*She pauses.*) You men!
WILLIAM (*sadly*). Pompous vanity is our weakness.
PAUL (*with foolish dignity, and breaking with a swaying drunken walk to* R.C.). Glad you're amused.
ROSEMARY (*still ready to be reconciled*). Paul, don't be silly!
PAUL. After spending five hours exchanging idiocies with that woman, you can ask me not to be silly!
ROSEMARY (*rising and crossing to the door* L.). Oh! You are a fool!

(*She exits* L., *slamming the door.* PAUL *stares after her half bewildered, half angry, then stares blankly out front.* WILLIAM *rises and breaks to* C. *below the rostrum.*)

WILLIAM (*waving his arm to indicate the Curtains*). Let's hide the poor chump.

(*The Curtains close. Lights Cue 9.* HELEN, *as her ordinary self, enters by the arch* R. *and crosses to* R. *of* WILLIAM, *who takes her left arm and leads her down* L.C.)

HELEN. We shall have to look at them now, somewhere in the middle of the next stage, which is constant quarrelling.
WILLIAM. Now wait a minute. (*Reflectively.*) Constant quarrelling is bad for both, of course, but I think that in this quarrelling stage the woman is better off than the man.

(WILLIAM *breaks off as* HELEN *turns to him and begins straightening his tie, brushing his hair back and generally trying to smarten up his appearance. She then takes him by his right ear and swings him round to face* JOYCE.)

HELEN. And that's supposed to be a clever one. Imagine what some of the rest are like. (*She releases* WILLIAM'S *ear.*)
JOYCE. He just doesn't know, dear. How could he?
WILLIAM (*severely and rather annoyed, breaking below* HELEN *to* R.C.). Instead of indulging in antics, I will produce a reason or two for my statement. The woman is better off because—first, an emotional outburst, a *scene* is less repugnant to her than it is to the wretched man, who will go to almost any length to avoid one. Secondly, the woman has a superior technical equipment and knows instinctively how to put the fellow in the wrong and keep him there, and has a diabolical skill in detecting the weak joints in his armour. (*He moves to the piano* R. *and leans against it.*)
HELEN (*crossing to* R.C.). The said armour consisting of solid plates a foot thick, of masculine vanity, conceit and self-complacency. (*She crosses to* L.C.) While the poor woman, her heart thumping away, her tummy tying itself in knots, has no armour and feels practically naked.

PHILIP. But I thought you liked to feel practically naked.
HELEN. Five minutes after he has (*she breaks to* C. *doing a funny walk*) stamped out of the house the man begins to forget about the quarrel, and by the time he has plunged into the day's business it no longer exists for him. But the woman lives with the quarrel all day and half the night, as if she were wrestling with a giant scorpion. She hears the angry voices hour after hour. Her whole world looks as if it has been torn into quivering strips by an earthquake. The very chemistry of her being . . .
WILLIAM (*breaking to her, taking hold of her right hand and kissing it*). Yes, yes, yes, my pet. An excellent speech. How well you do these things. We all enjoyed it. But I think we ought to be getting along. Let's have another look at them. (*He breaks above* HELEN *to his stool* L. *and sits.*)
HELEN (*crossing to her stool* R. *and sitting*). Here they are then. Typical!

EPISODE 5

The Curtains open to reveal PAUL'S *study.*

The room is the same as before, but the furniture has been struck and replaced by a modern desk on which are books, inkwell, blotter, papers, etc. An architectural blueprint hangs on the wall R. *There is a modern chrome stool at the desk.*

(*See the Ground Plan at the end of the Play.*)

PAUL *is sitting at the desk making a few casual notes. He is not working very hard and after a moment or two* ROSEMARY, *looking rather pale and strained, enters* L. *She crosses to the upstage end of the desk, above* PAUL, *and begins rather elaborately looking for something among the papers on it.*

ROSEMARY (*very politely, after a few moments of searching*). I'm sorry to disturb you.
PAUL (*with strained politeness*). That's all right. Can I . . . ?
ROSEMARY (*still searching vaguely*). No, no, no . . .

(*Her negatives get weaker, then she turns, crosses to the door* L. *and exits. After a moment or two, she re-enters, and moves to* C., *looking as if she has been in the room for hours.*)

You haven't seen my scissors—the large pair—have you?
PAUL (*half rising, very politely*). No, I'm afraid I haven't. Can I . . . ?
ROSEMARY (*looking around vaguely*). No. No. Sorry to disturb you, that's all.
PAUL (*resuming his seat*). No, that's all right. (*He goes on with his work.*)

(ROSEMARY *gives him a sharp, contemptuous look, turns and exits* L.)

WILLIAM. I don't quite see the point of this dodging in and out.

HELEN. She's giving him a chance to be human again and to say he's sorry, and then of course she'll say it's all her fault. But meeting this heavy politeness, she knows that the quarrel is still on.

WILLIAM. Why has the man to say he's sorry first? He nearly always has, you know.

HELEN. Yes, but once he does the woman is nearly always ready to be downright abject.

WILLIAM. Quite so. But why has he to start the ball rolling?

HELEN. It's a kind of tradition with us.

(*There is a pause.*)

WILLIAM. That is—very curious.

(ROSEMARY *enters* L. *and this time stands* L.C. *rather rigidly looking at* PAUL'S *back.*)

Back again. Different technique this time.

HELEN. Yes. She's still giving him a chance, but now she's hardening rapidly. The excuse to talk to him will be a telephone conversation that she's saved up for this moment.

ROSEMARY (*in a cold, polite tone*). I forgot to tell you that Mona Roberts rang up to ask if we'd dine with them on the fifteenth. Do you want to go?

PAUL (*rising slowly and taking off his spectacles*). Not particularly, (*he turns and moves* R.C.) I think he's rather a bore. But you like her, don't you?

ROSEMARY (*in the same tone as before*). Yes, but I can see her some other time. It's not essential that you should go and be bored.

PAUL. No, if you want to go . . .

ROSEMARY. I know how easily you are bored.

PAUL (*heavily*). Was that necessary?

ROSEMARY (*furiously*). Oh—don't be so pompous.

PAUL (*still heavily, folding his spectacles and putting them in his pocket*). Really, I don't see why I should be accused of being pompous just because I try to be decently polite.

ROSEMARY (*cold and contemptuous*). Don't you?

PAUL (*with more warmth*). No, I don't.

ROSEMARY. Well, what am I to say to them about the fifteenth?

PAUL (*impatiently breaking* R.). Oh—say what you like. What do I care?

ROSEMARY. What do you care about anything?

PAUL (*contemptuously*). What does that mean?

ROSEMARY (*contemptuously*). What do you think it means?

PAUL. I don't know. (*He turns his back on her.*)

ROSEMARY. No, of course *you* wouldn't. (*She turns her back on him.*)

(WILLIAM *and* HELEN *rise, both cross and meet* C. *below the rostrum, looking at* PAUL *and* ROSEMARY *in astonishment.*)

WILLIAM (*to* HELEN). Y'know, what's wrong with this is our horrible modern poverty of language. It's sheer misery to feel such sudden hate and despair and yet be so inarticulate.

HELEN. I agree. They'd feel ever so much better if they could let it rip.

WILLIAM (*breaking* L.). Then we'll let it rip for them. We'll make an Elizabethan job of it. Hold tight, girl! Blow, wind, and crack your cheeks.

HELEN. Rage, blow! You cataracts and hurricanes.

(PHILIP *plays a roll of thunder on his piano—Music Cue 13. The* LIGHTS *quickly dim to a Black-Out—Lights Cue 10.* HELEN *exits by the arch* R. WILLIAM *exits by the arch* L. JOYCE *picks up the theme on her piano, and both pianists continue to play throughout the following speeches.* PAUL *and* ROSEMARY *step down from the rostrum. The Curtains close.* PAUL *moves to the stool* R., *and sits.* ROSRMARY *moves to the stool* L., *and sits. There are some lightning flashes—Lights Cue 11.* WILLIAM *and* HELEN, *wearing cloaks, enter by their respective arches, mount the rostrum and meet* C. *The flashes cease and they are illuminated by two blue spots—Lights Cue 12.*)

(*In the grand manner.*) Oh—that I should be tied to such a
    pudding bag
Of dreary vanity and duller wit. A thing
Made up of braces, collar-studs and starch,
With hardly more red blood in it than drips
Out of the poor frozen joint from Argentine.

(HELEN *crosses below* WILLIAM *to* L.C. *of the rostrum.* WILLIAM *crosses above her to* R.C.)

WILLIAM. Imagine a cat five feet four inches high,
Take away its dignity and let it rage
With deep inferiority—and that's a wife.

HELEN. Why—hot-water bottles of the cheaper sort,
Bargains from Boots, bring me more comfort.
Two and fourpence at the nearest Odeon
Bring more romance or cheerful entertainment.

WILLIAM (*closing with* HELEN *and pointing to her*). You're
    Madam Nature's grim old conjuring trick.
Every man's disappointment—girl into wife.
I married a loving, ripe and merry lass.
To find myself keeping, at a rising cost,
A bitter woman who hates the sight of me.

ACT II] EVER SINCE PARADISE

HELEN (*moving and standing in front of* WILLIAM). And why?
Because I had a lover once
And now he's disappeared, and in his place
For me to live with, are a costing clerk, a
Lecturer, a stomach and a thirst.

(HELEN *breaks down off the rostrum and crosses to* R. *of the piano* L. WILLIAM *breaks down from the rostrum and crosses to* L. *of the piano* R. PHILIP *and* JOYCE *cease playing. There are more flashes of lightning—Lights Cue 13, which continue until the fall of the curtain.*

ROSEMARY
HELEN } (*together, and all pointing at* WILLIAM). Oh, hateful, pompous clown!
JOYCE

PAUL
WILLIAM } (*together, and all pointing at* HELEN). Oh, damned, malicious shrew!
PHILIP

(WILLIAM *and* HELEN *begin to quarrel.* PAUL *and* ROSEMARY *rise, point to each other and begin to quarrel.* JOYCE *and* PHILIP *rise, point to each other and begin to quarrel. There is a crash of thunder.*)

The CURTAIN *falls.*

ACT III

The setting is the same.

When the CURTAIN *rises,* PHILIP *and* JOYCE, *at their pianos, have already commenced playing the introduction—Music Cue 14. They go on brilliantly for some time, then* PHILIP *stops and rises. A moment or two afterwards,* JOYCE *also stops.*

JOYCE (*rising, annoyed*). What's the matter, darling?
PHILIP. Well, nobody's coming on or anything. What happens now? You see, it's exactly what I said. They can't make a third act out of it. All the critics will say " Not really a play at all, and even so it goes to pieces in the third act." (*He sits again at his piano.*)
JOYCE. Well, you're quite wrong. The third act's all right, and it's starting now. (*She sits again at her piano.*) Listen ! (*She pauses a moment, then begins to play a few bars of pseudo-Oriental, mystical music—Music Cue 15.*)
PHILIP. What's that muck for? Are they bringing on a bogus Oriental illusionist?
JOYCE (*as she continues to play softly*). No, this is the fortune-telling music. Mme Aurora who's just returned from the East——
PHILIP. Probably Clacton-on-Sea.
JOYCE. —to read palms and gaze into crystals.
PHILIP. Rosemary's consulting her, I suppose?
JOYCE. Yes. (*She stops playing.*) She and Paul have now arrived at the third stage, when each feels the other is hopeless and is ready to be consoled by somebody else. And of course Rosemary's having her fortune told.
PHILIP. Using her husband's money to find out if there is any other chap on the way.
JOYCE. What a noble mind you have, maestro.

(JOYCE *begins to play again, swelling out the theme, in which* PHILIP *joins in a mocking manner. Lights Cue 1.*)

EPISODE 1

The Curtains open to reveal a corner of Mme Aurora's tent.
  There is a bamboo cane table covered with a cloth C. *On it stands a glass crystal and an ashtray with a pipe resting in it.*
  (*See the Ground Plan at the end of the Play.*)

ACT III]   EVER SINCE PARADISE   59

ROSEMARY, *in outdoor clothes, is sitting in a chair* R. *of the table.*
HELEN, *as Mme Aurora, sits in a chair above the table. She wears an Oriental shawl, with grey hair showing under it, and probably large spectacles. She is studying* ROSEMARY'S *hand. After a moment or two,* PHILIP *and* JOYCE *cease playing.*

HELEN (*in a thick, common voice*). Yes, dear, I see you're married. Two children.
ROSEMARY (*hastily*). One.
HELEN (*quickly*). That's right, dear. One. I'm afraid you're not very happy. Nothing like so happy as you thought you was going to be. Of course, dear, your trouble is you're a lot more sensitive than people think—you've a very loving, sensitive nature, it's 'ere as plain as a pikestaff an' what's the result? The result is people close to you 'urt your feelings when they 'ardly know they're doing it. An' what else? You go an' trust people—for you've a trusting nature. I can see that—an' then they go an' let you down. Isn't that right?
ROSEMARY. Yes, it is. I can't imagine how you can see me so clearly.
HELEN. It's a gift, dear. Very few 'ave it, an' even then it needs a lot of development. (*She coughs.*)
ROSEMARY. Could you—tell me what's going to happen?
HELEN (*staring at* ROSEMARY'S *hand*). I see a tall man coming over the sea with love for you in his 'eart. You'll meet him soon, quite soon, an' he'll make you very 'appy. I see a journey —and a strange bed.
ROSEMARY (*withdrawing her hand*). What sort of strange bed?
HELEN (*darkly*). Never you mind about that, dear. (*She continues with a marked change of manner.*) And that'll be seven-and-sixpence, thank you, Mrs—er . . .

(JOYCE *commences to play the theme—Music Cue 16.*)

ROSEMARY (*rising hastily*). Oh, yes—of course. Thank you so much. Good morning.
HELEN. Good morning.

(ROSEMARY *turns and exits* R. HELEN *picks up the pipe from the table, puffs at it and blows out a cloud of smoke that has in it somehow her contempt for the credulous. The Curtains close. Lights Cue 2.* PHILIP *breaks in on* JOYCE *with some quick harsh music, calling across to her at the same time.* JOYCE *stops playing.*)

PHILIP (*pleased with himself*). Not bad, eh? Taxis . . . Street scene . . . (*He ceases playing.*)
JOYCE. What about this? (*She plays a heavy thumping tune in march time.*)
PHILIP. Now what's that?
JOYCE. Major Spanner on the way. (*She ceases playing.*)

PHILIP. Who's Major Spanner?
JOYCE (*loudly and cheerfully*). He was the wedding-guest, you remember, who'd known her for a long time and didn't think Paul good enough for her. An awful chump, if you ask me, but nearly every woman's got one of these faithful hounds tucked away somewhere. Keep the street going.

(PHILIP *resumes playing. As he does so* ROSEMARY *enters by the arch* R. *and eases down* R.C. *She looks at her watch, then glances at the space above the footlights as if it were a shop window, catches sight of something that interests her, tries it on, so to speak, then rejects it and is just turning away* L., *after giving another glance at her watch, when she sees* WILLIAM, *as Major Spanner, enter by the arch* L. *He is bronzed and trim, just back from the East.* WILLIAM *starts to cross* R. *They both look at each other as they pass, then pause, turn and recognize each other with delight. The Pianists cease playing.*)

WILLIAM (*with enthusiasm, raising his hat*). Why—Rosemary!
ROSEMARY (*equally pleased*). George Spanner!

(*They turn, close, and move down* C. *together;* ROSEMARY R. *of* WILLIAM. *They stand and talk in front of the imaginary shop window through which we see them.*)

How nice to see you again!
WILLIAM. Wonderful to run into you like this! Just goin' to ring you up, matter of fact.
ROSEMARY (*with mock severity*). You haven't been back ages and never told me?
WILLIAM. Of course not, my dear Rosemary. I only got in last night.
ROSEMARY. You didn't come to England at all, did you, on your last leave?
WILLIAM. No. (*He makes a slight break and looks away* R.) Haven't been here since your marriage. (*He turns back to her.*) You remember?
ROSEMARY. Yes. And I've missed you, George.
WILLIAM. Ho, ho. Like to believe that, but sounds a bit steep. I mean, (*he leans to her*) young married woman and all that.
ROSEMARY. But you're one of my very oldest friends, George, and of course I've missed you.
WILLIAM (*with embarrassment*). Very decent of you to say so, Rosemary. Of course, I've missed you no end. (*He turns away* R.) Fact is, that's why I stayed out East last leave. (*He turns to her.*) Felt I couldn't face it here with you—well—er—tied up elsewhere sort of thing.
ROSEMARY. George, is that true?
WILLIAM. Word of honour. I shouldn't have mentioned it, of course. Your fault it slipped out. Let's forget it.

ROSEMARY (*beginning to ease up* L.). But I don't want to forget it.

WILLIAM (*breaking to up* L. *above* ROSEMARY). Look here, I suppose you're busy an' crowded with engagements, eh? No chance of joining me in a spot of lunch, eh?

ROSEMARY (*turning and facing* WILLIAM). I'd love to.

WILLIAM (*taking hold of* ROSEMARY'S *left arm and moving to the arch* L.). Good show!

(PHILIP *and* JOYCE *commence to play softly—Music Cue 16a.*)

Now look here, I'm out of touch and you know all the places. Where do you suggest we go?

(WILLIAM'S *voice dies away as he and* ROSEMARY *exit by the arch* L. HELEN *enters by the arch* R. *as Mrs de Folyat. The music dies down and stops.*)

JOYCE. I'm sorry, Helen, but I think that outfit's all wrong for you.

HELEN (*moving to* R. *of the piano* L.). It's not meant for me. This outfit is for Mrs de Folyat—you know, the rich widow who talked to Major Spanner in the wedding-reception scene. She's given Paul another commission, after leaving him alone for several years, and now she's getting her claws into him. Paul and Rosemary are in the third stage now, you know.

JOYCE. Yes, I know. But what's she after, this Mrs de Folyat?

HELEN. Anything she can get, I think. But nothing very serious. If she can detach an attractive man from his wife and keep him playing around and coming to her for sympathy, she's quite happy. A sort of collector.

JOYCE. I know. And how I hate 'em.

HELEN. Yes, but men often like them.

JOYCE. Men'll like *anything*.

PHILIP. And so will women.

HELEN. I must see how the Spanner affair is progressing. (*She turns, crosses up* C., *mounts the rostrum and peeps through the Curtains to the inner stage. She then turns and speaks to* JOYCE.) Yes, yes. I think at any minute now she may throw a biscuit or a bone at his doglike devotion.

(*She breaks* R., *steps down from the rostrum and exits quietly by the arch* R. *Lights Cue 3.*)

EPISODE 2

The Curtains open to reveal a corner of a restaurant.
There is a small table C., *covered with a white cloth. On it are coffee-cups and glasses for two, an ashtray and a table-lamp.*
(*See the Ground Plan at the end of the Play.*)

There is a chair L. *of the table, in which* ROSEMARY *is sitting, and a chair* R. *of the table, in which* WILLIAM *is sitting. They have finished their meal and are smoking.* WILLIAM *takes a photograph in a leather travelling frame from his hip pocket and shows it to* ROSEMARY.

WILLIAM. Yes, this photograph you once gave me—you remember it, eh?
ROSEMARY. Yes, but that was ages ago. I'd only just left school. You don't mean to say *that's* the photograph.
WILLIAM. Yes, it is. I had this neat little folding—er—frame arrangement made for it, and take it everywhere. Been in some dashed queer places, (*he puts the photograph away in his hip pocket*) I can tell you.
ROSEMARY. But George, that's terribly touching. I'd no idea . . .
WILLIAM. No, no, of course not. I couldn't expect you to have. But er—well, I don't mind telling you now, Rosemary, it was quite a blow—had to take it right on the chin—when I came home last time and found you'd just got engaged to Weybridge. (*He pauses.*) Because I was going to say something pretty fierce to you myself.
ROSEMARY (*softly*). I'm sorry, George. (*She pauses and stretches her hand out across the table to him.*)

(WILLIAM *pats her hand enthusiastically.*)

Go on. Tell me some more.
WILLIAM (*patting her hand again more heavily*). Isn't much more to tell, really. Except this. Shouldn't have said anything now if I'd known you were happy. But now I know you're not, it's different. (*He pauses, leans back in his chair and then resumes fiercely.*) Good God, a wonderful little girl like you not being happy.
ROSEMARY (*half laughing*). But you're forgetting. I'm not a little girl and haven't been for years. Not only am I married but I'm a mother—nearly a matron.
WILLIAM. Nonsense! To me you're a little girl; (*he leans forward and pats her hand again*) my little girl.
ROSEMARY. Really, George. (*She pats his hand.*) I believe you've been taking a course or something. You say all the nice things I want to hear.
WILLIAM (*now patting her hand again*). You won't like this, though it's got to be said. You're not happy, are you? Weybridge doesn't realize what a lucky fella he is.
ROSEMARY (*quietly and sincerely*). It doesn't seem to be working somehow. (*She pats his hand.*)
WILLIAM. Queer thing. At your wedding too, some fool of a woman a friend of his, of course, told me what a clever fella

Act III]   EVER SINCE PARADISE

the bridegroom was. And I as good as told the woman there and then in my opinion you were worth ten of him, ten of him. (*He pauses.*) I've been uneasy in my mind ever since.

ROSEMARY (*affectionately*).   Poor George!

WILLIAM (*fatuously*).   Well, that's something. But—er—is that the best you can do?

ROSEMARY (*in a half comical whisper*).   No.

WILLIAM (*with doglike devotion in his stare, taking her hand and kissing it*).   A wonderful little girl!

(PHILIP *commences to play*—*Music Cue 17. The Curtains close. Lights Cue 4.* HELEN *enters by the arch* R., *wearing a light coat or something to suggest outdoors, but no hat. It is essential that she should look a rich, attractive woman. She crosses to* C. *below the rostrum.* PHILIP *ceases playing.*)

HELEN (*calling*).   Here I am, Paul.

(PAUL *enters by the arch* R. *and closes to* R. *of* HELEN. *He wears an ordinary lounge suit without hat or overcoat and carries a notebook and pencil.*)

Now then, this is what I mean. (*She points.*) Would it be possible to enlarge the wing that way? No, you can't see it properly from here. (*She takes his arm and leads him a few paces to* R.) This is better. (*She keeps her hand inside his arm.*) Now you see what I mean?

PAUL.   Yes.   It could be done.

HELEN.   Mind you, Paul, I wouldn't *dream* of letting anybody but you lay a *finger* on the house. You do understand that, don't you?

PAUL.   Yes.   That's very good of you.

HELEN (*turning so that they face each other*).   Paul—don't be so *professional.*

PAUL (*smiling*).   Sorry, Frances. But you see, it was a professional question you were asking me.

HELEN.   Oh—but I can't divide relationships into compartments like that. Don't forget—(*she releases his arm and moves a little away from him*) I'm a woman.

PAUL (*smiling and closing with her*). I'm not likely to forget that, my dear Frances. (*In a mock whisper.*) In fact, if I didn't think there were at least a couple of your housemaids watching us through a bedroom window, I'd probably behave—this very moment—very unprofessionally indeed.

HELEN.   You talk as if architects could be struck off the register, like doctors.

PAUL.   Oh—no, we can be trusted. If you don't make it too hard for us.

HELEN (*changing her attack*).   Paul, I think you're looking tired.

PAUL (*breaking* R.). I have been rather hard at it lately.

HELEN. Of course. A man in your position and with your genius has to *give* and *give*. We all understand that. (*She breaks to* L.C.) But it's obvious that wife of yours isn't looking after you at all.

PAUL. Well, as you know, we don't get on—and of course, now she isn't very much interested in my welfare.

HELEN (*with a fine show of indignation*). Paul, I think it's *monstrous*. To have no *intellectual* companionship, no deep store of sympathy, at home—that's bad enough—in fact, for a man of your kind it's the worst thing of all—but on top of that simply to neglect the most obvious duties a woman has towards a man—oh!

PAUL (*uncomfortably*). Well—there it is. (*He attempts to change the subject.*) Do you think you'd like . . .

HELEN (*breaking in, impressively, and closing with him*). Paul, I think I ought to meet your wife. Remember, I haven't seen her since your wedding and don't know her at all. You ought to bring us together.

PAUL (*alarmed*). I don't think that would work very well, would it?

HELEN. My dear. *Please* remember I'm a sensible woman of the world—and don't get into a silly masculine panic. There won't be any scenes. I'm a client—we've something to talk over—so you ask me to your home.

PAUL. All right, only don't blame me if you don't enjoy yourself.

HELEN (*taking his arm again and moving with him up* L.). Of course I'll enjoy myself. Better make it lunch, though, not dinner. Just the three of us. I'll look at my book and see if we can fix a date.

(HELEN *and* PAUL *exit by the arch* R. JOYCE *plays a few harsh chords—Music Cue 17a.*)

PHILIP. What on earth is that?

(JOYCE *ceases playing.*)

JOYCE (*grimly*). Just a brief sketch of the music for that lunch. (*She plays a few more notes, then stops again as* PHILIP *speaks.*)

PHILIP. Is it going to be like that?

JOYCE. It'll be worse than that. (*She resumes playing.*)

(WILLIAM, *as his ordinary self, enters by the arch* L., *and crosses down* R. JOYCE *ceases playing.*)

WILLIAM. Getting a bit tired of Major Spanner. Not a

ACT III]   EVER SINCE PARADISE   65

character that gives a fellow much scope. Where's Helen? Still doing Mrs What's-her-name? (*He breaks* L.)

PHILIP. Yes. Mrs de Folyat wants to meet Rosemary, so Paul's got to arrange a lunch.

JOYCE. If he'd any sense, of course, he'd have refused. The two women'll sit there, hating each other, and he'll be wretched. However, I like this third stage, with philandering just round the corner. I'm getting quite interested now.

WILLIAM (*moving down* L. *and addressing the audience*). Not much comment now, in my opinion. It's rapidly degenerating into ordinary theatrical muck.

PHILIP. That's what she likes.

JOYCE. It's what anybody likes. Let's see how they're getting on at that lunch.

WILLIAM. I'm against it. (*He turns and moves up* L.) Leave 'em alone.

JOYCE. Just have a peep.

(WILLIAM *mounts the rostrum, moves* C. *and stealthily peeps through the Curtains to the inner stage.*)

How's it going?

WILLIAM (*turning and quoting sombrely*). " Light thickens and the crow makes wing to the rooky wood."

PHILIP. Hamlet?

WILLIAM. Macbeth. And it's extraordinary—the way Shakespeare . . .

JOYCE (*breaking in impatiently*). Oh, never mind about Shakespeare now—I want to see what's happening at that lunch. It'll be over soon.

WILLIAM (*stepping off the rostrum and moving* L.). Over now, I think.

(WILLIAM *exits by the arch* L. *Lights Cue 5.*)

EPISODE 3

The Curtains open to reveal the entrance-hall of PAUL *and* ROSEMARY'S *home.*

The only furniture is a half-round table, with a telephone on it. (See the Ground Plan at the end of the Play.)

PAUL *is standing* C., ROSEMARY R. *and* HELEN, *who is just departing,* L. *They have their backs to each other and turn into the scene as the* CURTAIN *rises.*

HELEN (*with false gusto*). Thank you *so* much, Mrs Weybridge. (*She breaks down* L. *and in dumb show, applies lipstick and powder.*) It's been such a pleasure coming here and meeting you, especially after I've heard so much about you from your clever, clever husband.

ROSEMARY (*with obvious false geniality*). Awfully good of you to come, Mrs de Folyat. I hope you'll come and dine with us sometime.
HELEN. That would be *lovely*.
PAUL. I'll see you down to your car, (*he moves* L.) and then I must get back to the office.

(HELEN *exits* L.)

'Bye, darling.
ROSEMARY. 'Bye, darling.

(PAUL *exits* L.)

Of all the false, faked-up, smarmy, poisonous, man-hunters! It wouldn't be so bad if he'd found himself a *decent* woman! (*She turns to the telephone and lifts the receiver.*)
PHILIP (*to* JOYCE). You women always say that, don't you?

(ROSEMARY *dials a number.*)

JOYCE. Yes. We do.
ROSEMARY (*speaking into the telephone*). Is that the Sahib's Club? Is Major Spanner there, please?

(*The Curtains close. Lights Cue 6.* PHILIP *commences to play de Folyat music Music Cue 17b. After a few moments,* JOYCE *joins in with the Spanner music. After a few moments they stop.*)

PHILIP. Don't come in with that awful Major Spanner tune now. I'm playing the Mrs de Folyat music. (*He plays a few more bars and stops as* JOYCE *speaks.*)
JOYCE. I know you are, dear. But I don't particularly like the way you are playing it.
PHILIP. I was playing it very well.
JOYCE. Rather too well, I thought. I believe you are beginning to take an interest in that frightful woman.
PHILIP. I am. Very attractive type. And probably cleverer than she looks.

(WILLIAM *enters by the arch* L.)

WILLIAM (*crossing to* C.). Well, I lay six to four against her.
PHILIP. I'll take you. It's money for nothing. Paul hasn't a chance against that woman.
WILLIAM. Hasn't he? Well, I think she's going to learn that the situation is not quite as simple as she imagines. The relationship between a husband and wife, even though they may be quarrelling all the time, is never simple, and I think we'll find that Mrs What's-her-name de Folyat doesn't realize that and so plays the wrong card.
JOYCE. I'm delighted to hear it.

ACT III]   EVER SINCE PARADISE   67

WILLIAM. Well, let's see. But give her every chance. (*To the Pianists.*) Music! Atmosphere!

(WILLIAM *breaks to* L. *and exits by the arch* L. PHILIP *commences to play de Folyat music—Music Cue 17c. Lights Cue 7.*)

EPISODE 4

The Curtains open to reveal a corner of Mrs de Folyat's lounge. There is a plain wall backstage with two small wall tables R. *and* L. *against it, on which are bowls of flowers, and on one a bottle of brandy and two glasses. The fireplace is* R., *in front of which stands a coffee-table on which are a bottle of whisky, and some glasses. There is a sofa down* C. *The whole effect should be hard, with bright colours.*
(*See the Ground Plan at the end of the Play.*)

HELEN, *as Mrs de Folyat, in a loose semi-evening gown, is at the coffee-table* R., *checking the drinks, and is all expectant. She moves up* R. *and arranges the flowers in the bowl on the table up* R. PAUL, *dressed as in the last scene, enters* L. JOYCE *rises and leans across her piano to watch the scene.* HELEN *turns, crosses down* L.C., *takes* PAUL *by his hands and pulls him to* C. *below the sofa.*

PAUL. I came along as soon as I could. I was kept at the office until nearly nine.
HELEN (*all solicitude*). Poor boy! But have you had anything to eat?
PAUL. Yes, I had a quick bite at the club on the way here.
HELEN (*moving to the table up* R.). Drink then, eh? Whisky, brandy? (*She pours out some brandy.*) This brandy's supposed to be rather wonderful. Let me give you some. And sit back and relax. You poor boy. You must be so tired.

(PAUL *sits* L. *on the sofa and relaxes.* HELEN *turns and with the glass in her left hand moves to above the sofa and adjusts a cushion behind* PAUL'S *head. He reaches for her right hand and takes hold of it.* HELEN *immediately leans over and kisses him.* PHILIP *immediately ceases playing, rises and leans across his piano to watch the scene.* HELEN *hands* PAUL *the drink.*)

There, darling! (*She moves below the sofa and sits* R. *of* PAUL, *close to him.*)

(*They now look very cosy and relaxed.* PAUL *sips his drink.*)

PHILIP. She knows her stuff all right.
JOYCE (*sharply*). Sh-sh.
PAUL (*crossing his left leg over his right*). You're perfectly right, Frances. This is wonderful brandy.

HELEN. Well, my dear, I always take a little trouble and try to get the best of everything. I may not always look it, but, believe it or not, I'm rather a clever woman.

PAUL (*smiling and taking her hand*). You're a fascinating woman, and that's even more important. (*He kisses her hand.*)

(HELEN *smiles and cuddles up to* PAUL, *who lies back with his right arm around her.*)

HELEN. Well, we had our lunch.

PAUL (*not quite happily and withdrawing his arm*). Yes, we had our lunch.

HELEN. And of course, being a man, you loathed every minute of it, didn't you?

PAUL (*sipping his drink*). Yes, 'fraid I did.

HELEN (*soothingly*). Never mind. All over now. But of course I had to see for myself.

PAUL (*interested in his glass*). And what did you see?

HELEN. My dear! Why, of course, you're quite right.

PAUL (*rather stiffly and lowering his glass*). What do you mean? About Rosemary?

HELEN. Of course. Everything you'd told me about her—as well as everything you meant to infer—was, of course, absolutely right. She's completely wrong for you.

PAUL (*tonelessly, and uncrossing his legs*). Yes. (*He puts his empty glass down on the floor,* L. *of the sofa.*) I suppose she is.

HELEN. But—I mean—I saw that in two minutes. I can quite see how it all began, of course. A nice, fresh little thing. But now, you're quite right. You're growing all the time. She can't develop. In fact, like most women of her type, she's narrowing instead of broadening. It's not even a matter of being really *aware*—of being—shall we say—intellectual—but, of course, she's not even moderately intelligent. In fact, let's admit it, she's *stupid*.

PAUL (*who has liked this less and less*). You know, you really saw Rosemary at her worst today. I mean, we've been having rows and so on—and then I think she spotted something.

HELEN. Oh—but then—as I say, it didn't take me two minutes to *see*. She is *stupid*.

PAUL (*angrily*). She isn't stupid.

HELEN. My dear Paul, there's no need to be cross merely because I'm agreeing with everything you've told me about her.

PAUL (*sulkily*). I never said she was stupid.

HELEN. Not in so many words, perhaps. It takes a woman to do that. But you've told me she doesn't make an effort to understand you—she doesn't try to develop. And now that I've seen her for myself I'm merely telling you in one word why—because she's——

PAUL (*looking away to* L. ; *crossly*). Yes, yes, yes. You said it before.

HELEN. Paul, what's the matter?

PAUL (*turning to face her*). I suppose the matter—is that I don't enjoy listening to you sneering at my wife.

HELEN (*annoyed herself now*). Sneering! When I'm only . . .

PAUL (*cutting in sharply*). I know. You said that before too. Well, no doubt it's all very illogical, inconsistent and absurd, after all the rot I've talked, but there it is—*I don't like it.* (*He rises, breaks* L., *turns, and looks at her with a forced change of manner.*) I'm sorry, Frances, I've had a long day and I'm probably rather tired. I think I'd better go. (*He eases* L.)

HELEN (*cooling rapidly*). I think you had. I also think you're behaving very stupidly.

PAUL. No doubt that's the trouble with us Weybridges— we're *all* stupid people. Thank you for the brandy. Good night.

(*He exits* L. *hurriedly.* PHILIP *and* JOYCE *seat themselves and begin to play Music Cue 18. The Lights fade out slowly to moonlight—Lights Cue 8. The Curtains close.* PAUL, *wearing a light raincoat, enters by the arch* L., *as if walking home. He mounts the rostrum and crosses it to* R.)

(*Muttering angrily.*) Damned cheek talking about my wife like that! Just damned cheek. (*He breaks off the rostrum to down* R.) Rich, spoilt woman—say anything. (*He turns and crosses to up* C. *below the rostrum and then listens.*)

ROSEMARY (*off*). Darling . . . The lilac . . .

(*The Pianists are playing Chopin music.* PAUL *hears it.*)

Chopin . . . Perfect . . . Only three days . . . I love you.

PAUL. Rosemary!

(*He exits hurriedly by the arch* R. *Lights Cue 9. After a few moments, the curtain of the arch* R. *is drawn aside and* PAUL, *still in his raincoat, is seen standing in the alcove as if in a telephone box, with a telephone receiver in his hand.*)

(*Speaking into the telephone.*) Rosemary, listen, darling . . . Oh, it's you, Nannie, could I speak to Mrs Weybridge, please? . . . Gone away, well, if there's a note you'd better read it to me . . . Gone away for the week-end, perhaps longer, all right then, Nannie. If she does ring up would you tell her I've gone away too, and I might be back on Monday, and I might not.

(*The curtain of the arch* R. *closes. Lights Cue 10.* PHILIP *and* JOYCE *cease playing.*)

PHILIP. It's too bad she wasn't there, just when he was ready to make it up.

JOYCE (*rising*). Doesn't surprise me, though. That woman at lunch was the last straw, so she telephoned Major Spanner to take her away somewhere, for a nice little bit of consoling romance.

PHILIP (*showing more interest, rising and moving to* R.C.). Oh, that's it, is it? They've taken to the road, have they, probably under a false name? Fun in a Tudor Trust House, eh? Though I have my doubts about the Major.

JOYCE (*breaking to* L.C.). Oh, I don't know. I'm beginning to fancy the Major, though I think he'd need a lot of training. Not a week-end man at all.

PHILIP (*breaking to down* R.). The blatant cynicism of you women—ugh!

JOYCE (*indignantly*). And after the things I've heard you say.

(*Lights Cue 11.*)

EPISODE 5

The Curtains open to reveal a corner of a private sitting-room in a very Olde Worlde Inne.
The door is backstage L. *There is a window* R. *with a small table below it. There is a sofa* C.
(*See the Ground Plan at the end of the Play.*)

ROSEMARY, *in day clothes, is sitting* R. *on the sofa, looking rather forlorn and dubious.*

PHILIP (*turning and looking at the scene*). There we are. Ye Olde Tudor Inne with plaster beams. (*He moves to his piano and sits.*)

JOYCE. And he's taken a private sitting-room with the best double bedroom adjoining it. Well, well, well! (*She moves to her piano and sits.*)

(WILLIAM, *as Major Spanner, dressed in dinner clothes, enters up* L. *and moves down* L.C. *He has traces of a cold, which gets worse throughout the scene.*)

ROSEMARY. But, George, you've changed.

WILLIAM (*startled*). Changed? Same man you've always known. Loved you for years.

ROSEMARY. No, I mean your clothes.

WILLIAM. Oh, yes. Always like to change. (*He leans over the back of the sofa to her.*) Make a habit of it. (*He breaks to down* L.) Keeps a fella from getting slack, y'know.

ROSEMARY (*half vexed, half laughing*). But we want to be slack. That's why we've come here. Besides, I didn't bring any evening things with me.

WILLIAM. Oh—I see. (*He fiddles with his tie and moves* C.) Look odd, will it?

ROSEMARY. Of course it will. We'll have to have dinner up here.
WILLIAM (*rather disconcerted*). Oh—will we? Oh, I say. (*He moves to the sofa and sits* L. *of her*.) I've just commandeered a good table down there. Slipped down for a short drink before dining. (*He sneezes, sniffs a little, then rises and moves* L.) Fact is, that bathroom's damned draughty and I didn't notice it in time. Have to be rather careful after all these years in a hot climate.
ROSEMARY (*vaguely*). Yes, of course. Well, you'd better slip down again and tell them we'll dine up here.
WILLIAM. You don't think it would look odd, do you? (*He points to the door*.) I mean, you know what these people are.
ROSEMARY (*rather impatiently*). Well, if you like you can dine down there by yourself and I'll just have something on a tray up here. I'm not very hungry anyhow.
WILLIAM (*moving to the sofa and sitting* L. *of her*). Oh, aren't you? Oh, I say, that's rather a shame. Food here's pretty good, too. That's how I remember the name of the place.
ROSEMARY. I don't care. I didn't come here for *food*.
WILLIAM (*leaning away from her, rather embarrassed*). No, of course not. Neither did I, of course. (*He pauses*.) Happy, little girl?
ROSEMARY. Yes, of course, darling. I've been enjoying the lovely peace of it. To be quiet—with peace all round—lovely.
WILLIAM (*dubiously; laughing*). Yes, quite. Mayn't last, though.
ROSEMARY (*startled*). Why?
WILLIAM (*breaking into a laugh*). Got a big table all laid out down below (*he leans towards her*) and the head waiter told me it's for a crowd of Air Force blokes who make a night of it here every Friday. Probably won't be much peace and quiet when those lads get started. Ho-ho.
ROSEMARY. Yes, but I didn't mean *that*.
WILLIAM (*turning to her, seriously*). No, of course not. (*He leans back*.) Quite understand what you mean.

(*There is a pause*.)

ROSEMARY (*wistfully*). George, do you really love me?
WILLIAM (*rising, breaking* L. *and then turning to her*). Why, Rosemary, little girl, you know I do. (*He pats his hip pocket*.) Haven't I carried that photograph of you with me everywhere for years? Got it here now, matter of fact.
ROSEMARY. You don't want it now because you've got me. (*She stares at him speculatively a moment, then rises and faces him*.) You know, George darling, (*she kneels on the sofa*) I hope you realize that a photograph is one thing and a real live person is

quite a different thing. I mean, are you quite sure it's me—me myself—you really want?

WILLIAM. Why of course, Rosemary darling. I tell you, I've dreamed of this for years.

ROSEMARY (*stifling all doubts*). Darling! (*She holds up her face.*) Kiss me!

WILLIAM (*closing to her*). By Jove, yes. Just a second. (*He suddenly stops, turns away and sneezes violently.*) Oh—damn! Sorry! (*He sniffs and then blows his nose hard.*)

ROSEMARY (*impatiently, and rising*). Have you got a cold?

WILLIAM (*annoyed and apologetic*). Yes, beginning to look like it. Damn that bathroom. I felt a touch somewhere, too, coming down in the car. That's why I wanted the window closed. (*He breaks* L.) But you wouldn't hear of it.

ROSEMARY (*rather coldly*). I'm sorry. (*She sits* R. *on the sofa.*) I didn't realize you were so susceptible to colds.

WILLIAM. Well, a fella can't be years in a hot climate and then come back to this cold, damp hole—(*he moves very slowly up* L.) without . . . (*He just catches another sneeze, turns, moves to the sofa and sits* L. *of her, looking at her very gravely.*)

(*There is a pause.*)

ROSEMARY. What's the matter, George? Is it—something about us?

WILLIAM (*solemnly*). Oh—no. But I've just realized I didn't pack my little glass thing. For the nose, y'know.

ROSEMARY (*sadly*). No, George, I don't know.

WILLIAM (*solemnly, sitting very close to her and putting his right arm across her back*). Sort of nasal douche, y'know. Harley Street fella told me never to be without it here at home. First sign of a cold you fill it with a solution of common salt and bicarbonate, then use it night and morning. (*He goes through the motions of douching.*) Loosens and dissolves the mucus, he said.

ROSEMARY (*in a tiny voice*). Did you say the mucus, George?

WILLIAM (*solemnly*). Yes, Rosemary. (*He rises and moves* L.) And I've gone and forgotten the damned thing and it's too late now to buy one.

ROSEMARY (*sadly*). Yes, George, it's too late now to buy one.

(WILLIAM *gives another violent sneeze, fiddles with his shirt-cuff, takes out his handkerchief and mops his face.* ROSEMARY *suddenly bursts into a fit of hysterical laughter, rocking and sobbing with it, while* WILLIAM *sniffs, pats his nose and stares at her in amazement.*)

WILLIAM (*puzzled*). Look here, are you laughing or crying?

ROSEMARY. Both! Both! (*She rises with sudden decision and moves to him.*) Listen, George, do you know what we are going to do?

WILLIAM (*surprised*). Well—yes—I suppose .
ROSEMARY (*briskly*). No, you don't, so I'm going to tell you. One of us is going to drive back to town tonight, *now*, and the other is taking the early train back in the morning. Now, if you like you can stay here and enjoy your cold and let me go back in the car now. Or . . .
WILLIAM (*just stifling a sneeze*). But—but—I mean to say—what—I thought we were . . .
ROSEMARY. No, we're not, my dear. I like you very, very much, but all the rest of it is simply off. My mistake. And don't pretend not to be relieved because I know very well you are—and not just because you've got a cold, either. And if we both stay we'll only quarrel and feel silly afterwards. Now, do I go back in the car tonight, or do you?
WILLIAM. Well—if it's all the same to you—I think I'd like to get back—because if my cold . . .
ROSEMARY. I know—your little nose thing. That's settled then. Run down and get something to eat and I'll pack for you. Go on, there's a lamb. (*She almost bustles him to the door up* L.) And George! Remember! We've never been here. It never happened. All a dream. Oh—what name did you put in the hotel register?
WILLIAM (*at the door, still trying not to sneeze*). All I could think of was the name of an old C.O. of mine—terrible old stickler—(*he sneezes*) Smith.

(*He turns and exits up* L. ROSEMARY *moves to the sofa where she sits, half laughing, half crying. The Curtains close. Lights Cue 12.* JOYCE *plays a bar or two of the Major Spanner theme —Music Cue 19.*)

JOYCE (*ceasing to play*). All he wanted was to go on with his nice, safe little doglike devotion. A photograph to wag his head over when he'd had a few drinks, and not a real woman.
PHILIP. He's probably got two or three little brown wives in Banji-Banji. But I thought that bogus romantic devotion was just what you women wanted.
JOYCE. Not at all.

(HELEN *enters through the* C. *of the inner stage Curtains and stands* C. *on the rostrum.*)

HELEN. What we women want is something quite simple, and it's you men who make it all seem complicated. What we want is simply to be intensely real living people to the men we love. Nothing fancy at all—we get over that a year after we've left school not strange, romantic, glamorous figures—but just attractive and desirable real *people*. And your trouble is, whether you're romantics, sensualists, Don Quixotes, Don Juans, it's all the same—you won't let us be real people. You'll turn us into anything, dolls, goddesses, drudges, symbols, phantoms, rather than recognize us as our simple selves. And that's the honest truth.

(JOYCE *commences to play—Music Cue 20. Lights Cue 13. The curtain of the arch* L. *is drawn aside and* ROSEMARY *is seen standing in the alcove as if in a telephone box with a telephone receiver in her hand.*)

ROSEMARY (*speaking into the telephone*). Oh, Nannie, is Mr Weybridge there? . . . I see . . . All right, Nannie . . . (*She hangs up, lifts the receiver and begins savagely to dial another number.*)

(JOYCE *breaks into some staccato music and then stops abruptly as* ROSEMARY *speaks.*)

(*Into the telephone.*) Is that Fletcher, Fletcher and Coulson? . . . Is Mr Coulson there, please? . . . Mrs Weybridge. Say it's rather important . . . Oh, Mr Coulson, could I see you as soon as possible? . . . Well, it is really . . . Well, it's—it's (*hurriedly, but rather louder*) it's about a divorce.

(*The curtain of the arch* L. *closes. Lights Cue 14.* PHILIP *and* JOYCE *play a bar or two of mournful music.*)

HELEN. And there you are. That separated them.

(PHILIP *and* JOYCE *cease playing.*)

JOYCE. It's just the sort of dam' silly thing that would.
PHILIP. No doubt. But may I point out one important fact. If she hadn't been in such a hurry to ring up that solicitor . . .
JOYCE (*rising and moving* L.C.). Yes, yes, we know. But she felt she had to do *something*. I understand exactly how she felt.
PHILIP. There you are. You women . . .
HELEN (*cutting in*). Yes, we'll admit it's when we feel thoroughly upset, we *are* inclined to do the first thing that comes into our heads.
JOYCE. Oh Lord—yes.
PHILIP. Quite so. Whereas—if you'd only take it easy, just turn things over, enjoy a little quiet reflection . . .
JOYCE (*cutting in*). You've been taking it easy, turning things over, and enjoying your little quiet reflection ever since I've known you.
PHILIP. I prefer to ignore that type of remark.
JOYCE (*mocking his tone*). He prefers to ignore that type of remark.
PHILIP (*annoyed*). Oh—do shut up!
HELEN. Hoy hoy! It's not you two we're doing but Paul and Rosemary. Now of course, it was months—and horribly

Аст III]   EVER SINCE PARADISE   75

dreary months—before they found themselves together in the solicitor's office.

JOYCE. Yes, it would be. (*She breaks to her piano* L.) But don't show us any of those dreary months. (*She sits at her piano.*)

(WILLIAM, *carrying two chairs, enters through* C. *of the inner stage Curtains. He sets the chairs* C. *at the downstage edge of the rostrum and he and* HELEN *sit,* WILLIAM L. *of* HELEN.)

WILLIAM. No, no, we can imagine.

HELEN. In any case, they ought to be back in that solicitor's office by now. Joyce! Philip!

(JOYCE *and* PHILIP *commence to play—Music Cue 21. Lights Cue 15.*)

EPISODE 6

The Curtains open to reveal the solicitor's office, exactly as Act I, Episode 1.

PAUL, *as before, is moving about, crossing to* L. *and* R. *like a man kept waiting for an unpleasant appointment. After a moment,* ROSEMARY *is heard speaking off* L.

ROSEMARY (*off*). Oh, in here. Thank you!

(ROSEMARY, *wearing the same clothes as in Act I, Episode 1, enters* L. *She stops and stares at* PAUL, *who looks very embarrassed.*)

PAUL (*with an effort, now standing* R.C.). I'm afraid this is—er—rather embarrassing—Rosemary.

ROSEMARY (*with a similar effort*). Yes—Paul—I'm afraid it is. (*She moves to the chair, sits, and looks away from* PAUL.)

PAUL. Well, it's not my fault. I had a note from Coulson asking me to be here at half-past three—to answer some questions about the—the divorce.

ROSEMARY (*with a tiny voice*). Yes, so had I.

PAUL (*restlessly, moving to up* C.). Oh, I say—monstrous thing for Coulson to do——

(PHILIP *and* JOYCE *fade the music out and cease playing. The lights begin to fade—Lights Cue 16.*)

—asking us both here at the same time. Shows you how blankly insensitive these lawyers are. (*He crosses* R. *and turns.*) Typical lawyer's trick this. Damn Coulson!

ROSEMARY (*faintly*). Oh—I don't think—it's—perhaps (*Her voice dies away.*)

PAUL. What?

ROSEMARY. No—nothing.

PAUL (*closing to* R. *of the chair*). Look here, I'll go and wait out there. (*He indicates the door* L.)
ROSEMARY. No—it . . . (*She makes a movement as if to halt him.*)
PAUL (*moving to the door* L.). Don't mind a bit.

(*They stare at each other uncertainly and miserably. The lights on the inner stage are nearly out, and the lights on the main stage also begin to dim.* JOYCE *and* PHILIP *rise from their pianos.*)

JOYCE (*moving to* L.C.). It's just as it was before. In another minute he'll go out, and that poor girl will start crying.
PHILIP (*moving to* R.C.). And if we're not careful, we'll find ourselves arguing about it as before, and then we'll be shown how they first met, and (*he moves up* R.) it'll all go round and round.
JOYCE (*moving up* L.). It's not good enough.
PAUL (*quietly and indignantly*). I couldn't agree with you more.
ROSEMARY (*rising; in the same tone as* PAUL). It's really Helen's fault—and William's.
PHILIP (*his voice fading*). Well, my dear, let them settle it.

(*He turns to the arch* R. *and exits.*)

JOYCE (*her voice fading*). And themselves too, if they can, darling.

(*She turns to the arch* L. *and exits. The Curtains close. The main stage lights have dimmed to Black-Out except for a single fire-spot illuminating* WILLIAM *and* HELEN *who are sitting at the front edge of the rostrum as if by a fireside.* HELEN *speaks quietly, as if concluding a long story.*)

HELEN. So there they were. Paul, like a fool, went out, and poor Rosemary sat there crying. Of course, she'd asked the solicitor to send for them both at the same time, in the hope that seeing her again, Paul might have discovered he was still in love with her. (*She pauses.*) William, are you listening?
WILLIAM. Yes, I'm listening. But I'm thinking too.
HELEN. No doubt. But I don't believe you were listening.
WILLIAM. Yes, I was. The last thing you said was that she hoped he was still in love with her. Well, he is. And he's only got to run into her anywhere outside that solicitor's office, and he'll show her he is.
HELEN. I'll tell her about that. Then she'll make sure he does run into her. But what were you thinking about—those two?
WILLIAM. No. About two other people.
HELEN (*who knows at once*). Oh!
WILLIAM (*slowly*). Two people—rather older and more mature

—and perhaps cleverer in some ways—than those two, who also fell in love, got married, and went galloping away to happiness—only, of course, to find the usual hurdles and jumps and obstacles—losing the first excitement of possession, disagreeing about friends . . .

HELEN (*quietly*). Complaints about being taken for granted or neglected, and jealousy when other men and women were specially attentive.

WILLIAM (*quietly*). And then a whole fog of cross-purposes . . .

HELEN. And each of them wearing their pride like blinkers . . .

WILLIAM. And so, instead of clearing the hurdles and reaching the long flat stretch where they could canter home in trust and affection, they turned aside, they broke—they got divorced.

HELEN (*with concealed emotion*). One of them—didn't seem to mind very much—behaved as if it were true what he'd said when —when they were quarrelling—that marriage wasn't right for him.

WILLIAM. He was a fool—and a liar. But he didn't know enough then. And those were the silly easy days when people were busy deceiving themselves. Now he knows that life is hard, and the years are slipping by and soon the nights will be longer and lonelier and friends will vanish, and where there might have been love to the end, not excitement and passion and possession, not rockets and stars, but the steady glow of the fire, there will be darkness—and nothing. (*He pauses.*) She can't understand that yet.

HELEN (*half laughing, half crying*). Oh, can't she? You ask any woman living alone!

WILLIAM. But she needn't live alone.

HELEN. She prefers to.

(*There is a pause.*)

WILLIAM (*turning to her*). I'm giving myself a last chance, Helen.

HELEN. Why do you say that?

WILLIAM. Because this—being friends, all so gay and matey and cool—doesn't work any longer for me. I've tried hard but I can't make it work. So if this is all, I'm going away.

HELEN (*alarmed at once*). Going away? Where?

WILLIAM. I don't know—but a long way.

HELEN (*hastily*). You're not going without me.

WILLIAM (*turning to her joyfully*). Helen!

HELEN. No, wait, William. I agree with everything you've said and I've felt it too. But it's not good enough. I'm a woman—and not an insurance against a lonely old age. Say it —or never talk like this again.

(*There is a pause.*)

WILLIAM (*with great sincerity*). My dear, I love you—I love you with all my heart—and I ask you to forgive me—and marry me again.

HELEN. Oh—my darling—there's nothing to forgive—and I love you too—and, of course I will.

(*They embrace, and then after a moment she withdraws and looks at him, half laughing, half crying.*)

But, darling, making all that fuss and getting divorced—and then marrying again—they'll say we don't know our own minds.

WILLIAM (*sturdily*). Well, we do.

HELEN. They'll laugh at us.

WILLIAM (*roundly*). Let 'em laugh.

(*Lights Cue 17.*)

EPISODE 7

The Curtains open to reveal the back wall of a drawing-room.
Backstage C. *is a long trestle table, covered with a white cloth. On it are bottles of champagne in silver buckets, glasses, plates of sandwiches, etc.*
(*See the Ground Plan at the end of the Play.*)

PHILIP *is standing* R.C. *holding two glasses of champagne. On his* L. *is* JOYCE, *also holding a glass.* ROSEMARY *and* PAUL, *now both in evening dress, are standing* L.C. ROSEMARY *holding a glass, and* PAUL *on her* L., *holding two glasses. The curtains in the arches* R. *and* L. *are drawn aside, to show the alcoves, each with a pedestal with a bowl of flowers on it. A great burst of laughter comes from the four on the inner stage as the Curtains open. The laughter is friendly and not at all malicious.*

PAUL (*handing* WILLIAM, *who is* L. *of him, a glass of champagne*). Well, you're a bright pair. Ask us here to celebrate with you —and then go off into a corner.

(PHILIP *hands a glass of champagne to* HELEN, *who is* R. *of him.*)

WILLIAM (*grinning*). Sorry, old boy!

(ROSEMARY *and* JOYCE *break to the table up* C.)

ROSEMARY. And you haven't even congratulated Joyce and Philip. (*She picks up a plate of sandwiches from the table, turns, moves down to* L. *of* PHILIP *and offers it to him.*)

(PHILIP *refuses the sandwich with a smile and a shake of his head.*)

HELEN (*to* PHILIP). I hope you'll be very happy, Philip. I'm sure you will.

PHILIP. Thank you, Helen. I had to do something to make her play in tune.

WILLIAM (*crossing below* PAUL *to* L. *of* ROSEMARY). I don't know that in the long run marriage makes anybody very happy. (*He takes the plate of sandwiches from* ROSEMARY.) But then the single life doesn't make anybody very happy either. (*He crosses below* PHILIP *and* ROSEMARY *and offers the plate of sandwiches to* HELEN.) The fact is, (*he turns and crosses to down* L., *handing the plate back to* ROSEMARY *as he passes her*) nobody in his senses *can* be very happy.

HELEN. Don't start philosophizing now.

WILLIAM. No, my love. (*To* JOYCE.) My congratulations, Joyce!

JOYCE (*breaking down* L.C. *to* R. *of* PAUL). Thank you, William! I'm so tired of seeing him look bleary-eyed that I decided I'd better marry him to try and clean him up.

WILLIAM (*sternly*). For that, get back to your piano.

(JOYCE *steps down from the rostrum and moves to her piano* L.)

HELEN (*to* PHILIP). And you to yours.

(PHILIP *steps down from the rostrum and moves to his piano* R. *They all have their glasses of champagne in their hands and* ROSEMARY *still holds the plate of sandwiches*.)

ROSEMARY (*holding up her glass*). Well, here's to all of us

ALL (*ad lib., holding up their glasses*). To all of us.

(*They toast each other and drink, the three couples looking and smiling at each other.*)

WILLIAM (*moving to* ROSEMARY *and taking a sandwich*). Mind you, the sexual life, as even Shelley had to admit, is a cheat. (*He moves* L.)

JOYCE (*sardonically*). Are you telling us?

WILLIAM (*munching away cheerfully at the sandwich*). It's been a cheat ever since Paradise.

PHILIP. It has.

HELEN. It takes us women in just as it does you men.

ROSEMARY. Worse, I expect.

WILLIAM (*broadly now*). But to share the cheat together—with humour and kindness . .

HELEN (*smiling at* WILLIAM). With trust and deepening affection . .

WILLIAM. Is to put up a tent not too far from the shining gates.

(WILLIAM *and* HELEN *step down from the rostrum.* WILLIAM *moves to* L.C. *and* HELEN *to* R.C.)

ROSEMARY (*closing to* PAUL). That's true. And I only hope you'll all be as happy as Paul and I have always been.

PAUL (*too heartily*). Well, I suppose we've been exceptionally lucky—but there it is—never even a really serious misunderstanding.

ROSEMARY (*sweetly*). We said from the first we'd take care never to quarrel.

(PHILIP *and* JOYCE *seat themselves at their pianos.*)

HELEN. Well, I must say, my dears . . .

WILLIAM (*to* HELEN, *with irony*). I don't think we can do better than follow their wonderful example.

(*At this*, PHILIP *and* JOYCE *commence to play—Music Cue 22.* HELEN *and* WILLIAM *toast each other and then begin to move up stage on to the rostrum to meet* PAUL *and* ROSEMARY.)

The CURTAIN *falls.*

FURNITURE AND PROPERTY PLOT

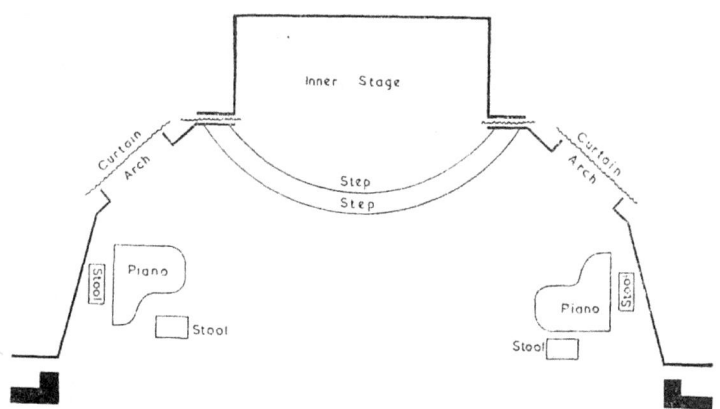

On the main stage throughout the play:
  2 pianos.
  2 piano-stools.
  2 stools.

ACT I

Episode 1

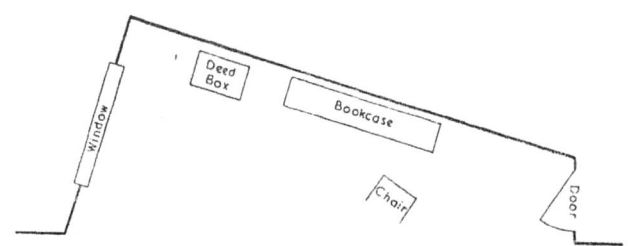

On Stage.—Bookcase.
     Chair.
     Deed-boxes.

Personal.—PAUL : spectacles.

EVER SINCE PARADISE 83

Episode 2

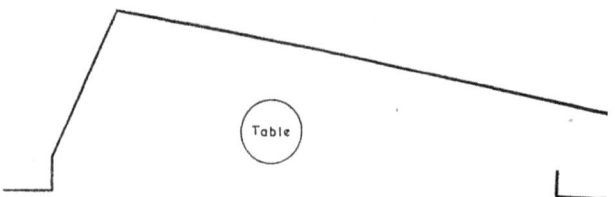

On Stage.—Round table. *On it:* tray, decanter of sherry, 3 sherry glasses, ashtray, cigarette-box.

Episode 3

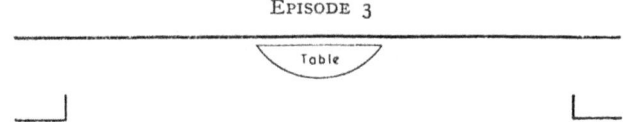

On Stage.—Hall table. *On it:* card tray, newspaper.
Personal.—WILLIAM: spectacles.

Episode 4

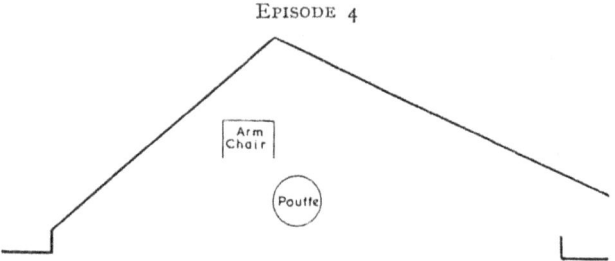

On Stage.—Armchair. *On it:* cushion.
    Pouffe.

Episode 5

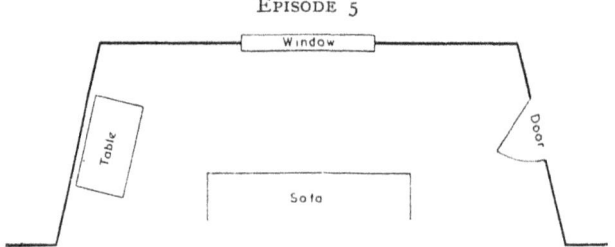

On Stage.—Sofa. *On it:* cushion.
    Table. *On it:* bowl of flowers.
    Curtains at window.
Personal.—WILLIAM: cigar-case containing cigar, matches.
    PAUL: cigarette-case containing cigarettes, matches.

Episode 6

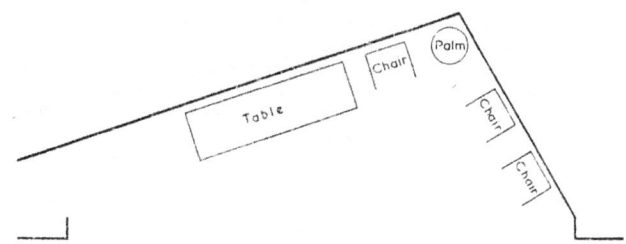

On Stage.—Palm stand with palm.
        3 chairs.
        Long trestle table. *On it :* 8 champagne glasses, 4 whisky glasses, 2 champagne buckets containing bottles of champagne, wedding-cake on stand, 3 plates of sandwiches, plate of pies.
Off Stage R.—Champagne glass (HELEN).
        Champagne glass (WILLIAM).
Personal.—WILLIAM : top hat containing confetti, watch, umbrella handkerchief in pocket containing confetti.

Episode 7

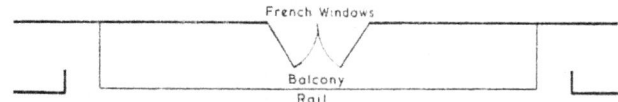

ACT II

Episode 1

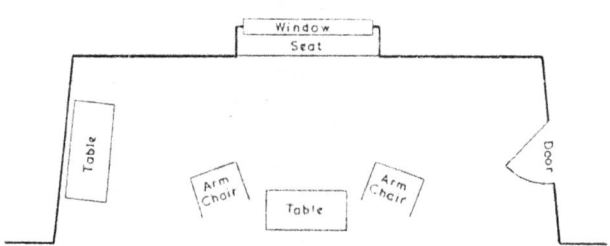

On Stage.—Table. *On it :* telephone, box of cigarettes.
        2 armchairs.
        Coffee-table. *On it :* ashtray, glass.
        Book on chair R.
        Newspaper on chair L.
Personal.—WILLIAM : pipe, newspaper.
        PHILIP : newspaper.
        PAUL : matches.

EVER SINCE PARADISE   85

Episode 2

Strike: glass from table C.
Set: bowl of flowers on table C.
  box of chocolates on chair R.

Episode 3

Strike: bowl of flowers and box of chocolates.
Set: glass on table C.

Episode 4

Strike: glass from table C.
Set: on table C., newspaper.
  on table R., bottle containing tot of whisky.
  2 whisky glasses.
Off Stage L.—Silver salver. *On it:* cocktail-shaker (full), 3 cocktail
  glasses (PAUL.)
  Book (ROSEMARY).
Personal.—WILLIAM: cigar, watch.

Episode 5

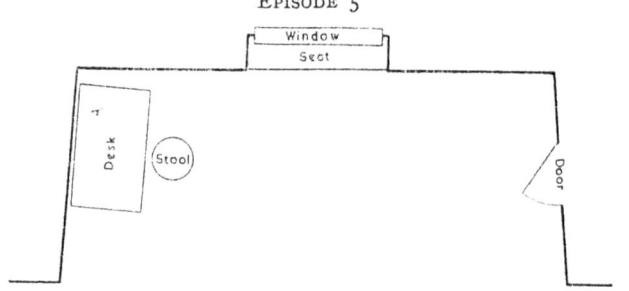

On Stage.—Modern desk. *On it:* blotter, pen tray, inkstand, lamp,
  books, pencil, large open book, notebook.
  Stool.
Personal.—PAUL: spectacles.

ACT III

Episode 1

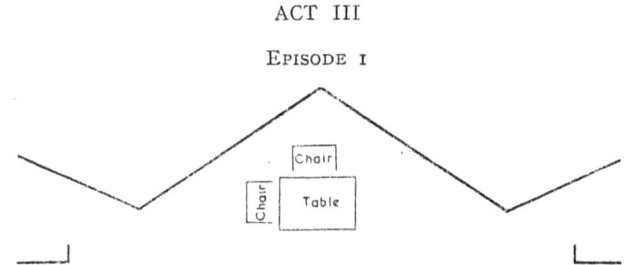

On Stage.—Bamboo table. *On it:* crystal, ashtray with lighted pipe in
  it, tablecloth.
  2 cane chairs.

Episode 2

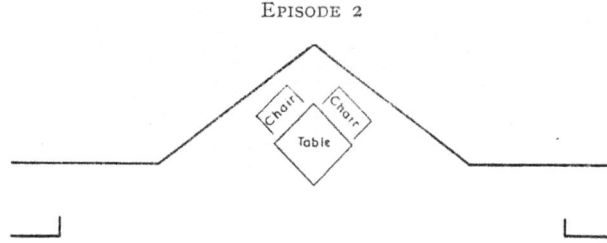

On Stage.—2 chairs.
    Table. *On it :* white cloth, ashtray, coffee-pot, 2 cups and saucers.
Personal.—WILLIAM : walking-stick, leather travelling photo-frame in hip pocket.
    PAUL : Notebook and pencil.

Episode 3

On Stage.—Hall table. *On it :* telephone.

Episode 4

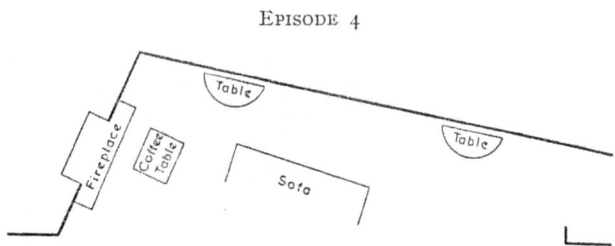

On Stage.—Sofa. *On it :* cushions.
    2 wall tables. *On them :* bowls of flowers, brandy bottle and glass on table up R.
    Coffee-table. *On it :* decanter of whisky, 2 whisky glasses, ashtray.
    Telephone in R. alcove.

Episode 5

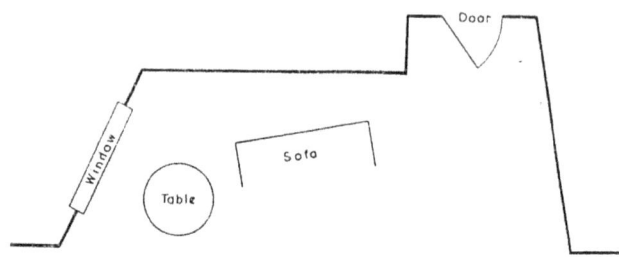

On Stage.—Sofa.
        Table. *On it:* bowl of flowers.
Personal.—WILLIAM: handkerchief.
        Telephone in L. alcove.

Episode 6
As Act I, Episode 1.

Episode 7

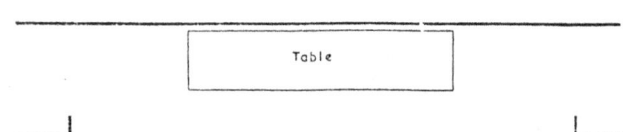

On Stage.—Trestle table. *On it:* 6 champagne glasses, white tablecloth, champagne buckets containing champagne, plates of sandwiches, pies, cake, pair of candelabra.
        Pedestals with bowls of flowers on them, in arches R. and L.

LIGHTING PLOT

THE lighting needs to be in two sections, one for the main stage, and one for the inner stage.

ACT I

Cue 1. *At rise of* CURTAIN.
   All lights for both stages to full.
Cue 2. HELEN: "You'll see. Joyce! Philip!"
   Check main stage lights to out.
Cue 3. WILLIAM: "I say, this is too bad . . ."
   Bring up main stage lights.
Cue 4. HELEN: "But she seemed to know at once."
   Check main stage lights to ¾.
Cue 5. HELEN: "I don't believe anybody knows."
   Bring up main stage lights.
Cue 6. WILLIAM: "Saying good-bye in the hall."
   Check main stage lights to out.
Cue 7. ROSEMARY: "Good night . . ."
   Check inner stage lights to ¼ leaving spot on ROSEMARY.
Cue 8. WILLIAM: "No, no, no . . ."
   Bring up main stage lights to full.
Cue 9. HELEN: "—but to dance."
   Check main stage lights to ½.
Cue 10. HELEN: "—she's ever called him Paul
   Bring main stage lights to full.
Cue 11. HELEN: "—with his point of view."
   Bring inner stage lights to full.
   Check main stage lights to out.
Cue 12. ROSEMARY: "Dear Paul!"
   Bring main stage lights to full.
Cue 13. WILLIAM: "There is nothing silly about it."
   Check main stage lights to out.
Cue 14. HELEN: "—for you're a very lucky girl."
   Bring main stage lights to full.
Cue 15. PHILIP: "Lights!"
   All lights fade to out except moonlight spot on PAUL and ROSEMARY.
Cue 16. ROSEMARY: "I love you."
   Check moonlight spot to out.
Cue 17. *Curtains open on Episode 6.*
   Bring inner stage lights to full.
Cue 18. WILLIAM: "Join you, I think."
   Bring main stage lights to full.
Cue 19. WILLIAM: "This one I think."
   Check main stage lights to out.
Cue 20. *Curtains open on Episode 7.*
   Check inner stage lights to out.
   Bring in moonlight spot to cover PAUL and ROSEMARY ON balcony.

EVER SINCE PARADISE

Cue 21. HELEN *enters* R.
    Bring on moonlight spot on HELEN at $\frac{1}{4}$.
    HELEN : " —give me that Mediterranean moon."
    Bring up moonlight spot on her to full.
Cue 22. WILLIAM *enters* L.
    Bring on moonlight spot on WILLIAM at $\frac{1}{4}$.
    WILLIAM : " Spill it and spread it, boys . . ."
    Bring up moonlight spot on him to full.
Cue 23. WILLIAM : " —his sword at Eden's gate."
    Bring on moonlight spots to cover JOYCE and PHILIP.

ACT II

Main and inner stage lights up to full to open.
Cue 1. JOYCE : " It's the beginning of a lament for women."
    Check lights to $\frac{3}{4}$.
Cue 2. WILLIAM : " Better get back on the job."
    Bring lights back to full.
Cue 3. PHILIP : " Lights ! "
    All lights Black-Out.
Cue 4. PHILIP *plays chimes on the piano.*
    All lights up to full.
Cue 5. HELEN *exits.*
    All lights Black-Out.
Cue 6. PHILIP *plays chimes on the piano.*
    All lights up to full.
Cue 7. JOYCE : " We all do it."
    All lights fade to out except a single pink spot illuminating ROSEMARY.
Cue 8. ROSEMARY : " It will be a beautiful . . ."
    All lights up to full.
Cue 9. WILLIAM : " Let's hide the poor chump."
    Check inner stage lights to $\frac{3}{4}$.
Cue 10. HELEN : " You cataracts and hurricanes."
    All lights Black-Out.
Cue 11. WILLIAM *and* HELEN *exit.*
    Lightning flashes from floats.
Cue 12. WILLIAM *and* HELEN *meet on the rostrum.*
    Bring in two spots to illuminate them.
Cue 13. HELEN : " A stomach and a thirst."
    Lightning flashes from floats.

ACT III

All lights full up to open.
Cue 1. JOYCE : " What a noble mind you have, maestro."
    Check main stage lights to out.
Cue 2. HELEN *puffs at pipe.*
    Bring main stage lights up to full.
Cue 3. HELEN : " —at his doglike devotion."
    Check main stage lights to $\frac{1}{2}$.
Cue 4. WILLIAM : " A wonderful little girl."
    Bring main stage lights up to full.
Cue 5. WILLIAM : " Over now, I think."
    Check main stage lights to $\frac{1}{2}$.
Cue 6. ROSEMARY : " Is Major Spanner there, please ? "
    Bring main stage lights up to full.
Cue 7. WILLIAM : " Music ! Atmosphere ! "
    Check main stage lights to out.

Cue 8. PAUL : " Thank you for the brandy. Good night."
      Fade lights to moonlight.
Cue 9. PAUL : " Rosemary ! "
      Fade all lights to Black-Out except illumination in alcove R.
Cue 10. PAUL : " —and I might not."
      Bring all lights up to full.
Cue 11. JOYCE : " —things I've heard you say."
      Check main stage lights to out.
Cue 12. WILLIAM : " —terrible old stickler—Smith."
      Bring main stage lights up to full.
Cue 13. HELEN : " And that's the honest truth."
      Fade all lights to Black-Out except illumination in Alcove L.
Cue 14. ROSEMARY : " —it's about a divorce."
      Bring all lights up to full.
Cue 15. HELEN : " Joyce ! Philip ! "
      Check main stage lights to out.
Cue 16. PAUL : " —for Coulson to do."
      Start slow fade of all lights commencing with inner stage.
      Finish with main stage lights to out by—
      JOYCE : " —if they can, darling."
      A single fire-spot is left on, illuminating WILLIAM and HELEN.
Cue 17. WILLIAM : " Let 'em laugh."
      All lights up to full.

www.ingramcontent.com/pod-product-compliance
Ingram Content Group UK Ltd.
Pitfield, Milton Keynes, MK11 3LW, UK
UKHW021844210426
5322IPUK00022B/452